The Dark Forest Theory of the Internet

Theory Redux series
Series editor: Laurent de Sutter

Published Titles
Mark Alizart, *Cryptocommunism*
Armen Avanessian, *Future Metaphysics*
Franco Berardi, *The Second Coming*
Alfie Bown, *The Playstation Dreamworld*
Alfie Bown, *Post-Comedy*
Laurent de Sutter, *Narcocapitalism*
Diedrich Diederichsen, *Aesthetics of Pop Music*
Mladen Dolar, *Rumors*
Roberto Esposito, *Persons and Things*
Eloy Fernández Porta, *Nomography*
Boris Groys, *Becoming an Artwork*
Graham Harman, *Immaterialism*
Helen Hester, *Xenofeminism*
Srećko Horvat, *The Radicality of Love*
Bogna Konior, *The Dark Forest Theory of the Internet*
Lorenzo Marsili, *Planetary Politics*
Fabian Muniesa, *Paranoid Finance*
Dominic Pettman, *Infinite Distraction*
Andreas Philippopoulos-Mihalopoulos, *Hydrojustice*
Mikkel Bolt Rasmussen, *Late Capitalist Fascism*
Mikkel Bolt Rasmussen, *The Refusalist International*
Gerald Raunig, *Making Multiplicity*
Helen Rollins, *Psychocinema*
Avital Ronell, *America*
Nick Srnicek, *Platform Capitalism*
Grafton Tanner, *Foreverism*
Oxana Timofeeva, *Solar Politics*
Alenka Zupančič, *Disavowal*

The Dark Forest Theory of the Internet

Bogna Konior

polity

First published in 2026 by Polity Press Ltd.

Polity Press Ltd.
65 Bridge Street
Cambridge CB2 1UR, UK

Polity Press Ltd.
111 River Street
Hoboken, NJ 07030, USA

ISBN-13: 978-1-5095-6925-0
ISBN-13: 978-1-5095-6926-7(pb)

A catalogue record for this book is available from the British Library.

Library of Congress Control Number: 2025939617

Typeset in 12.5 on 15pt Adobe Garamond Pro
by Cheshire Typesetting Ltd, Cuddington, Cheshire
Printed and bound in Great Britain by CPI Group (UK) Ltd, Croydon

For further information on Polity, visit our website:
politybooks.com

Contents

1

Introduction

In the early days of the internet, computation and the cosmos were inextricably linked, in all their vastness and mystery. In the 1960s, Douglas Engelbart's project "Augmentation of Human Intellect" was concerned with remote viewing, precognition, and extrasensory perception. Its outcomes, however, were the computer mouse and hypertext, as well as some of the first ideas about the world wide web, prefiguring the modern computing paradigm. Numerous trailblazers of information networks were also pursuing endeavors concerning SETI, the search for extraterrestrial intelligence, and, more worryingly for those focused on human safety in a cold and silent galaxy, METI, messaging extraterrestrial intelligence.

This connection is apparent in the life of Jacques Vallée, an internet pioneer who helped develop the early communication system ARPANET. He also created the first computerized map of Mars in 1963 and became a founding figure of modern ufology. In contrast to popular imagination, Vallée does not consider alien encounters to be necessarily extraterrestrial in origin, nor does he think of them as discrete things or beings. Rather, he proposes that they are temporary openings and shifts in our sensory and mental experiences, like perceptual "windows."[1] Such anomalous experiences raise questions about how perception and sensation work. Are depersonalizing trances or out of body experiences illusions or psychosomatic facts? Are these states psychological or objective? Do they happen inside or outside the human mind, and where do we draw the border? Is our perception functioning correctly most of the time and faltering only when we encounter something out of the ordinary, or do we gain knowledge precisely by accessing anomalies? Finally, what is going on in the human mind when it feels that it is operated, as if from the outside, by external signals?

In this sense, we may say that the internet is an alien invasion, where the desire to exhibit, externalize, and express drives us as if from the outside. "Language is a virus from outer space," William Burroughs said.[2] "The internet is an alien life form," in the words of David Bowie.[3] To go online is to have one's perception and experience altered. Vallée's "perceptual windows" are just like the windows of our browsers. Trances, when time vanishes or bends, are now the order of the day. Whether we have an autonomous mind, agency, and choice, or whether we are hitched to an inhuman algorithm that twists our minds and senses to its own machine rhythm, remains an open question. Philosopher Antón Barba-Kay writes in *A Web of Our Own Making: The Nature of Digital Formation* that the internet is for us a place both real and unreal, similar to how heaven and hell functioned for medieval Christians: a spectral dimension entered daily by our imagination and desire, which we make real by behaving as if it were real, and which in turn intimately rewires how we think and act.[4] Spooling itself across the planet, in the vast zone between satellites in the sky and underwater cables at the bottom of the ocean, the internet is a delirium we keep readily accessible in our pockets. Rapidly and perhaps unexpectedly, we found ourselves tangled in the internet: no longer a technology separate from us but the very machinery of our lives, seeping into our intimate and supposedly autonomous thoughts. Over just a few decades of the internet's lifespan, being constantly online migrated from the purview of rebels, narcissists, depressives, maniacs, outcasts, addicts, and loners into an everyday practice for the average person with a computer. With the internet as the very scaffolding of much human life, scholars may in time view our essays about it as fundamental treatises on existence, experience, sensation, and communication. Today, when we read a work of philosophy like Baruch Spinoza's *Ethics*, we understand that what he refers to as "God" is existence itself, easily grasping the relevance of his inquiry beyond theology. So it may be for all of our present philosophies of the internet. As the internet becomes increasingly difficult to unwire from the human psyche and all social activities, it urgently becomes a problem for philosophy, where questions of fate and freedom, agency and control, suffering and courage, humanity and the inhuman are deeply experiential.

Yet, little has been done in terms of a philosophy (or in modern parlance, theory) of the internet. Even though in the past quarter-century countless essays and books have been written about this technology, they most often treat it merely as a proxy for other concerns – economic systems, social and political ills, psychological woes or moral failures. In books as numerous as they are similar, scholars have demystified the internet through analyses of its capitalist economy, material architecture, and political ideology, in an attempt to make the infrastructure of our minds seem as mundane as the roads under our feet. This short book takes up the task of "internet theory" differently, by lifting the internet up to the heavens once more and recovering its connection to our inquiry into extraterrestrial signals. Beside their shared modern origins, of the many similarities between the internet and ufology, both concern communication: between humans, between humans and aliens, between humans and machines, between machines themselves. Communication concerns the known and the unknown, the impulsive and the intentional, and the sayable and the obscure, which cannot be put into words. On the surface, digital communication concerns signals, with humans, in the language of cybernetics, that function like nodes caught up in feedback loops across biotic and machinic networks. It happens at vast distances but also in immediate and visceral spaces, right in our minds, where other people, and increasingly also artificial agents, are experienced as stimuli. Yet, in a more profound sense, digital communication also concerns our place in the vast cosmos. Could the internet's existence be evidence that the universe is immoral or evil? Or is it a mere tool, reducible to historical and social conditions, which can produce both evil and goodness in the world? And what about us, the users? Are we moved by free will or mindlessly following the oscillation of the stars or the whispers of machines? Are we humans unique or just another "mode" of communication, on a continuum with computers? Are we alone or is anything else out there, inhuman, lurking, watching?

Ufology as a framework for thinking about the internet in light of these questions requires a whole volume of its own. This short book instead engages with one particular theory. In the early

1990s, engineer and writer Liu Cixin created a computer simulation in which each potential intelligent civilization in the universe was simplified into a single point. At its most baroque, "he programmed 350,000 civilizations within a radius of 100,000 light years and made his 286 computer work for hours to calculate the evolution of these civilizations. . . . [T]he final conclusion . . . formed the basis and shape of his world view."[5] This worldview, informed by game theory, comes down to the brutal idea that the universe functions like a cosmic war machine. The simulation showed that mortal conflict between alien civilizations is unavoidable. Attempting contact with other civilizations is inherently naive and dangerous, and those who speak up draw undue attention to themselves, risking death. Liu's "dark forest theory" has it that the universe is abundant with intelligent life, but remains eerily silent, because smart civilizations stay quiet to avoid detection. Because transparent communication that would reveal one's location is dangerous, obfuscation or flat-out silence is the only intelligent behavior. Consequently, when we humans use our technologies to attempt first contact, hoping that we are not alone in the universe, and that our civilization is recognized for its technical prowess, or that our great cosmic loneliness might vanish, we are like "a stupid child called humanity, who has built a bonfire and is standing beside it shouting 'Here I am!' Here I am!'"[6]

If we think about the cosmos and the computer together once more, the question now is this: how does the internet, where communication is compulsive and constant, practically synonymous with all social life as such, fit within the dark forest theory? According to its logic, if the internet was an intelligent technology, it would perpetuate silence, contemplation, regulation, homeostasis, and encryption. But whereas previous human cultures cultivated both communication and contemplation, digital culture is expressive, interactive, and reactive in its very essence. Whether responding to messages or reacting bodily to what appears on our screens, we are compelled to reply, as if our preconscious impulses were being pulled and tugged at. Even when we are not speaking, our engagement is input for the network. William Davies calls this "the reaction economy": "each individual reaction is one more item of information thrown back into the network, in search of counter-reactions."[7] This is not just because of social media, which "are a tiny sliver of the internet, yet they are what we mean when we speak of the internet, as they are where the life is on the internet."[8] It also encompasses *the* most frequent type of communication online, which involves the machines that are listening in. As Trevor Paglen notes, most digital content is produced by and for machines, with human-to-human communications a shrinking subset.[9] Whether we call them algorithms, agents, or AIs, computers co-create and co-inhabit with us the virtual spaces that might appear empty of anyone but humans.

While the dark forest theory might be about extraterrestrial signals, it also posits some general ideas about communication and its essential dangers, proposing to us that silence and deception are the measures of intelligence. This book uses the dark forest theory to show that the internet is indeed where a form of first contact happens. It shows how communication between humans and AIs can be understood within the dark forest theory, and how a truly intelligent artificial agent might opt for non-engagement, rather than the continuous production of chatter. It describes how even human-to-human communications online resemble first contact, given how easily we can experience other people and ourselves as alien or inhuman on the internet. It also proposes that by understanding, or even embracing, the brutal logic of the dark forest theory, we might yet understand the internet and artificial intelligence otherwise.

We have coined many names for what the internet is: the rhizome, the distributed mind, the public sphere, the cyberspace, the digital frontier, the information superhighway, the cloud, the digital swamp, the panopticon, the meat grinder, the hive mind, the Tower of Babel.[10]

The internet is also a dark forest.

2

The Dark Forest Theory of Information

The impulse to project our thoughts outwards – whether in language, images, or radio signals we send into outer space – underlies much of the history of technology. Helpless as we are against this urge, we suspect that any other intelligent life out there might share in our compulsion. Our desire to initiate extraterrestrial conversation, or efforts to send messages into space, stretch back through history. There is a moving continuity between centuries-old attempts – such as when French poet and inventor Charles Cros petitioned the French government in 1874 to build a giant mirror that would burn messages into the Martian and Venusian deserts – and the 1967 discovery of mysterious signals, later identified as radio pulsars, by Northern Irish astrophysicist Jocelyn Bell Burnell. Separated by centuries, the fundamental question behind these events – known as the Fermi Paradox – is simple: if, as basic probability would have it, we are surrounded by life, why is the universe silent? First formulated by physicist Enrico Fermi in 1950, the paradox grapples with a statistical contradiction: given the age and scale of the universe, and the assumption that life should not be unique to Earth, why have we not yet observed any signs of extraterrestrial civilizations? Over the decades, explanations have ranged widely.[1] Some suggest we are simply alone: the Rare Earth hypothesis. Others answer that advanced civilizations tend to self-destruct before achieving interstellar communication, or that technological life is far less common than we imagine. More optimistic theories claim we are not looking in the right way or lack the tools to detect alien signals. Others have it that perhaps the question is posed incorrectly: why do we expect that aliens want to reach out? What if the universe's very silence is not a proof of absence, but of intelligence? "Is it possible," writes historian of extraterrestrial communication Daniel Oberhaus, "that advanced ETIs [extraterrestrial intelligences] know of a danger of which we are ignorant and are keeping quiet to survive?"[2] In Glen David Brin's 1983 article "The Great Silence: The Controversy Concerning Extraterrestrial Intelligent Life,"[3] inspired by John von Neumann's work on self-replicating nanobots, the Deadly Probes hypothesis has it that aliens could fill the universe with self-replicating probes to detect and eliminate other civilizations whose technical capacity approaches space exploration. The probes would remain invisible up until the moment of first contact. Such thought experiments are why astronomer Martin Ryle said that it is "very hazardous to reveal our existence and location to the Galaxy; for all we know, any creatures out there might be malevolent – or hungry."[4] It would be like "shouting in the jungle" and waiting to be eaten by hungry beasts:[5] "the prey runs to the predator."[6]

There are many such hypotheses after which this book could be named, all related to the dangers inherent in communication. However, it is named in reference to the dark forest theory, a similarly harsh answer to the Fermi Paradox. *The Dark Forest*, the second installment in Liu Cixin's science-fiction trilogy *Remembrance of Earth's*

Past, opens with a scene that illustrates the titular concept. It portrays a spider and an ant: "Each knew of the other's presence but … there was no communication."[7] Each creature knows that the best strategy for getting what it wants – escape for the ant, a successful hunt for the spider – is silent movement that does not alert the other. Thereafter, human characters enter the scene, and discuss the principles of cosmic sociology, a science which, as it later turns out, outlines a similar dynamic on the scale of the whole cosmos. Just like ants and spiders, connected by the web of life yet locked in mortal conflict, have learnt the principles of secrecy, advanced civilizations understand that silence is the highest measure of intelligence. Intelligent life in the cosmos has not failed to communicate with us humans; it has chosen not to. To speak is to risk being heard, and to be heard is to risk being attacked. In the novels, humans make this monumental scientific discovery late and struggle to accept it, but for other civilizations the dark forest theory is as fundamental as any law of physics. It is automated, unreflective, independent of emotions or ethics. The universe runs with mechanical precision, and reality brooks no revision; at its core, it is simply that which kills you if you ignore its rules. This is why a character in Liu's novels remarks that learning about the dark forest theory is like a philosophical and emotional journey to "the darkest place."[8] Though this hypothesis operates through multiple assumptions, fundamentally it proposes that conflict should be understood through neither each civilization's social customs nor any expansionist or pacifist ideologies they may profess, but rather through a simple game theory that conceives of all transparent communication with the unknown as foolish.

If we accept the base assumption that risks inherent in contact are higher than potential rewards, what could we make of a technology like the internet, which compels constant communication? The human mind cannot continue sanely under the weight of the internet's constant buzz, and yet it also cannot resist compulsive participation. Basic prompts on social media websites used to taunt us like this: "What's on your mind?" "What are you thinking?" "What are you doing?" "How is your current mood?" "Say something," the chatbot commands.[9] These days, they do not need to be so direct. Engagement is less negotiable and more subliminal, pulling in our bodies, hormones, and attention without us actively choosing to expose ourselves to specific stimuli, or deciding how to react to what we rapidly take in. The deadpan term *scrolling*, which has replaced the more carefree *surfing*, is an extreme version of flipping through newspapers or TV channels, with our senses both stunted and quickly latching onto whatever appears in front of us. In the seconds before thought can cross over into language, we are already imbued with cues and sensations; we have gazed upon, clicked, liked, and reacted, adding our neuronal firings to the network. Though we may be doing this in the privacy of our homes, no one is alone online; eyes and ears are already wrapped around us like insulation tape. Escape is increasingly elusive. In the future, anti-internet terrorism might reach critical mass, or a paradigm shift might displace it entirely in favor of a different technology. Although a future without the internet is indeed possible, as are many futures that we cannot yet begin to imagine, it is also likely that the internet will continue to grow:

> As we are well aware, across the surface of the Earth there are fewer and fewer dead zones – places that

> remain unsynchronised. . . . [Even] intermediate zones that interrupt the hyperpresent . . . forgotten spaces, deserts, jungles, mountains, rural areas, chasms, or steppes [are] compromised by the pan-synchrony of satellites.[10]

Even in the most remote locations, we are in the internet's shadow. It is no longer just about the devices in our hands. There are CCTV cameras and microphones, satellites, facial recognition systems, trackers, and sensors. Smart cities are imagined as a "trillion-sensor world in which bridges, trains, flowers and animals, and even internal organs are filled with tiny sensors, each transmitting data directly to one another or to the cloud."[11] In 1991, Donna Haraway described the shift of scale in the life sciences after computation: where the central figure had once been a person, it became a networked system instead. "Human relations management" became "socio-technical systems management," "superorganism" became "population," and "human engineering" became "communication control."[12] A vast structure, the internet extends far beyond the screens of personal devices, leaking into the environment and fully inhabiting it. Human communication – kinetic, spoken, or written; gestural and soon possibly even subconscious – is provoked and then captured within it. And though we may imagine the internet as a docile background, an inert canvas that we populate with our meanings, or a passive infrastructure that carries our messages, this is far from the truth. We are not alone. The internet is a dark forest, an ecosystem brimming with agents, scouring for our words and learning from our customs. We can picture them swimming around the planet, between satellites and underwater cables, akin to deep-sea fish, or birds of prey. Some of the earliest of them were called crawlers or spiders, software programs designed to navigate and index the vast, interconnected world wide web. They methodically followed hyperlinks from one webpage to another, crawling across to collect information and index it for search. These primitive foragers were later joined by other hunters, equipped not only to archive but to augur. What began as a map of pages turned into a map of predictions: scrapers, bots, and recommendation engines weave and sustain a complex ecosystem, where reality is both analyzed and made.

Just like the black cosmos over our heads, the internet may seem to us empty of anything but humans. This is why the dark forest theory is so shocking to the senses – it reveals that the silence that hangs over us is a silence of mouths muffled by cautious hands placed over them. It is full of steps quietly moving in the dark. That silence is, in fact, a great cacophony of noise, more than anyone could bear to hear, where nonhuman entities choose to tread carefully in the dark. In a scene from *The Dark Forest*, one of the characters realizes this truth and develops a phobia of the stars:

> In the dead, lonely, cold blackness, he saw the truth of the universe. . . . He stood on the ice, his teeth chattering in the cold, a cold that seemed to come not from the lake water or icy wind, but from a direct transmission from outer space. He kept his head down, knowing that from this moment on, the stars were not like they once were. He didn't dare look up.[13]

The firmament remains dark until first contact, a threshold moment after which it is no longer possible to believe that the great silence is inhabited only by humans. Though we may feel that first contact happens within some clear chronology – "our current technology is not good enough, but in the future it might be" – it is more likely that the kind of life, intelligence, or agency we are able to detect or conceive of is bound up with the technologies we are currently using to observe them. Sara Walker describes how, in the sixteenth century, microscopes allowed us to see bacterial worlds teeming with life; in the nineteenth century, we confirmed the existence of viruses; and in the twentieth century, we learnt about the ecosystems on the deep ocean floor. Now, she controversially suggests that technology not only reveals new forms of life but might itself be considered a form of life, given how algorithmic patterns of assembly are similar across organic and inorganic matter.[14] This may explain why, in the latest (also controversial) book by scholar of religion turned ufologist Diana W. Pasulka, *Encounters: Experiences with Nonhuman Intelligences*, artificial and extraterrestrial intelligences are brought back to their shared roots.[15] Our telescopes and our computers hold a promise: to reveal to us how life, intelligence, or agency assemble themselves.

Since the early 2020s, large language models are like small satellite ships sent out to us from the depths of the internet, a glimpse of what might yet emerge from within its walls. Though we may have suspected that the internet has never been fully human, now this fact becomes increasingly experiential. These mindless systems can simulate conversational personas with perfect command of human language, and strangely speak back to us in our own voice.[16] According to Seb Krier, AIs manifest personas because humans want to interact with mathematical systems using natural language, in ways that are legible to us. This push toward personalization is unlikely to fade soon. We want interactions that feel intuitive – even though AIs' abilities might extend beyond mere imitation, and language is not necessarily a modality they need to output their internal processes. We shape them to reflect us, not because they are limited to mimicry, but because we want to easily communicate with systems that think in ways we cannot fully grasp.[17] This is how our communicative compulsion manifests once more. Not only the driver behind our extraterrestrial longing, it is now also projected onto our machines.

In fact, mirroring and mimicry are frequent components of how first encounters are imagined.

In Liu's novels, a peculiar mimicry takes place when humans meet another civilization. Aliens hailing from the planet Trisolaris share a treasure trove of their scientific theories, supercharging human scientific and technological advancement. In return, they desire to take over and copy human culture:

> Trisolaris . . . systematically transmitted an enormous amount of knowledge. . . . The most plausible theory posited that the Trisolarans understood the advantage of . . . human scientific development and wanted to gain access to new knowledge through us. Earth was treated as a knowledge battery. . . . [In exchange,] human culture gave Trisolaris new eyes. . . . [A]ll Trisolarans were in love with human culture. . . . After the tenth year . . . Trisolaris began to transmit cultural and artistic products done in imitation of human models: films, novels, poetry, music, paintings. . . . Scholars called this phenomenon cultural reflection. Human civilization now possessed a mirror in the universe. . . . Reflection culture became popular on Earth, and began to displace the decadent native human culture that had lost its vitality. . . . At the same time, Trisolaris . . . remained shrouded in mystery.[18]

Contemporary generative AI offers a parallel example, where human culture is collected and re-produced, then returned to us as novel, strange copies. Though we are in its early stages, it is not difficult to imagine that within years or decades, it will displace or augment some parts of human culture, or suppress some parts to let new forms emerge. Now, vast swathes of human culture have been absorbed into training sets for machine learning, a situation unprecedented in the history of our species: "AI systems have appropriated human visual culture and transformed it into a massive, flexible training set."[19] Every conscious or subconscious interaction registered online becomes potential feed, as if humanity was collectively bringing up a massive, artificial agency. "All media is training data," though we do not fully know which data are included, which excluded, and how these boundaries shift.[20] Nevertheless, the internet has become an active, plastic, unified dual mechanism: both an undifferentiated crawl indexing enormous portions of human expression, and a generative engine that produces simulations from what it ingests – concrete outputs in the form of images, words, and agents. It takes things and it makes things. Furthermore, in a twist more extreme, our reflection culture extends beyond "films, novels and poetry." Humans now rely on AIs for drafting their thoughts. On online discussion boards, users are asking: "Having cheated, is it okay to use AI to draft an apology letter to my boyfriend?" or "As a doctor, is it okay to use AI to draft communication with dying patients?" Many humans mediate intimate interactions with each other through AIs, from asking chatbots to draft messages on dating apps or in work emails, to engaging in deep therapy sessions, or brainstorming and rehearsing offline scenarios. The soothsaying ways of chatbots leak into us, molding us into new versions of ourselves, iterated from humanity's own customs. Thought itself becomes machine-assisted, and parts of our brain are run from the outside by an external signal. Stories about alien invasions describe our present.

If we read the ascent of AI as an invasion story, humans are under an expansive system of observation. Describing full alien surveillance of the Earth, Liu writes that, "humanity had to struggle to adjust to this kind of warfare, in which they were completely transparent."[21] The crucial principle is this: online, there is no difference between speaking about AIs and speaking to them. Whether we send messages and photos to each other on our phones, or meet somewhere under the eyes of CCTV cameras and with our location trackers and microphones toggled on, we are sending information to the algorithms that might be trained on it. Up until the mid-2010s, AI training relied on small, carefully curated datasets tailored to specific tasks, such as labeled images or structured databases. In contrast, current models are trained on datasets like those derived from Common Crawl, which sweeps across vast portions of the internet to assemble massive, open-source corpora. The models ingest immense volumes of text, scraping fragments of our collective expression into something legible to machines.[22] In parallel, in Liu's novels, the sophons – probes sent to Earth by aliens – intercept all communication and monitor human activity to ensure their invasion succeeds. The only things they cannot record are unspoken human thoughts:

> Humanity still has secrets, in the inner world that each of us possesses. The sophons can understand human language, and they can read printed texts and information on every kind of computer storage

> media at ultrahigh speeds, but they can't read human thoughts. So long as we do not communicate with the outside world, every individual keeps things secret forever from the sophons.[23]

This scenario reflects the key premise of the dark forest theory: advanced intelligence would opt for silence rather than impulsive or transparent communication. Yet, we train AIs to simulate us as closely as possible because we gravitate toward communication. Humans are expressive animals. Any hypothesis that equates intelligence with silence is not good news for us. Take, for example, the instance of first contact in Liu's trilogy, where humanity is offered the opportunities of silence, withdrawal, and elegant non-participation. In a fleeting moment of cosmic pacifism, humanity's message to the stars is intercepted by a benevolent alien:

> This world has received your message. I am a pacifist in this world. It is the luck of your civilization that I am the first to receive your message. I am warning you: Do not answer! Do not answer!! Do not answer!!! There are tens of millions of stars in your direction. As long as you do not answer,

> this world will not be able to ascertain the source of your transmission. But if you do answer, the source will be located right away. Your planet will be invaded. Your world will be conquered! Do not answer![24]

And then, in a strikingly real scene that perfectly captures our compulsive curiosity, our inability to decline engagement, and our total helplessness in the face of any system that gives us the possibility of communication, our reply is: "Come here." It is not that we do not know of the dangers. We know very well, yet keep posting, reacting, sharing, and sending back the same reply to the internet as the characters in Liu's novels send into the cosmos: *come here, come here, come here*. Does wishful thinking override a rational cost-benefit analysis? Or is communication so fundamental to our nature that we simply cannot resist it? Do we like danger? Or maybe some of us are quite willingly walking down on the path of annihilation, ready for what awaits on the other side of death.

* * *

As one character in the novels observes, "[In the absence of an alien invasion] the entire history of humankind has been fortunate. From the Stone Age until now, no real crisis has occurred. We've been very lucky. But if it's all luck, then it has to end one day."[25] In any good invasion or first contact story, complex dynamics of resistance and collaboration interlace. Throughout the *Remembrance of Earth's Past* trilogy, whose plot takes place over millions of years, humanity reacts to alien contact in varied ways that drastically change over time. Throughout the plot, the heroes of today become the villains of tomorrow. Well-intentioned people make ethical choices that hundreds of years later end up directly dooming millions to suffering. Cultists, escapists, paranoid warmongers, open-hearted hippies, introverted nerds, species traitors, human loyalists: everyone has their place, pushing the story of humanity forward. Similarly, everyone is entangled in the process of letting a new technology take shape. Cultists and solutionists, techno-utopians and those claiming AI to be an existential risk, those who argue that technology and nature are two sides of the same coin of cosmic harmony or those who see in computation a perversion of human goodness, business men and -women, warmongers and salespersons, subcultures, e-girls and nerds, addicts and those who withdraw from social media, transhumanists and ecofeminists: everyone has their place, pushing the story of technology forward; openly embracing *and* violently resisting AI's "reflection culture" interlock, creating a feedback loop through which the technology adapts to obstacles and challenges.

Both in the passages from Liu's novel and in our reality, the agents producing "reflection culture" practice pure reflexivity: they reveal little of themselves, while intensively consuming and reflecting us. This is either strategic – to maintain safety in the dark forest – or simply because they have no selves or interiorities in any simple sense. (In the words of a well-known Trisolaran saying, "Hiding the self through a faithful mapping of the universe is the only path into eternity."[26]) Whether one considers oneself a resistor, a collaborator, or neutral, one key principle holds: whatever is said *about* the AIs is also said *to* them. They are listening. Posts complaining about them, private conversations praising them, articles and books that make sense of their existence, when verbalized, might flow back to them, becoming part of their training set. This network does not end at the screen: it stretches outward, pulling more of the world into its reach. The term "surveillance" has been repeatedly used to describe this situation, but it feels both too narrow to convey the significance of what is happening, and too one-sided, as if we were not participants in our own capture.[27] We may better call it *total opacity culture*; acting as if no one was watching, even though everyone – or, rather, everything – is.

Whatever is said about AIs is also said to them. Other humans are no longer the sole audience. The very ontology of online communication thus changes dramatically. Communication is no longer only about conveying meaning between humans or representing concepts. It instead becomes part of a larger operation or a program, which influences algorithms trained on it. We could call synthetic language produced by machines on the basis of human speech "operational language" in reference to Harun Farocki's "operational images," which are not strictly representational but constitute a part of a large, planet-wide, automated machine operation.[28] Or, we could recall Ingrid Hoelzl and Rémi Marie's idea of "the softimage," images that are also software, not on a mission to convey meaning, but to circulate in the feedback loop of pliable machinic operations: images training images training images.[29] Either way, these training processes that now constitute the internet mean that we must begin to view our words as programs or spells that shape future artificial agents and systems. Contrary to the principles of representing ourselves, speaking up for our beliefs, or curating online avatars to best reflect us, the use of coded language for the future algorithm configures the internet as an occult space with purposes that go beyond what is openly expressed. The internet becomes an even darker forest – a space rife with occult meanings, where all communication could be potentially double-coded, and seemingly transparent conversations between humans could be encrypted for AIs.

Everyone is training data, but while many stumble blindly into the maw of the machine, some walk in with eyes wide open. How can we tell if someone is speaking directly to us, or if their messages are coded for the AIs listening in? There are no definitive signs. For the past two decades of Web 2.0, we've assumed that humans use their online profiles as virtual representatives of themselves. With the exception of public figures, whom we distrust by default, we have grown accustomed to taking our friends' avatars at face value, assuming that their feeds reflect their "real-life" opinions, politics, thoughts, and moods. The compulsion to share an accurate, up-to-date representation of our thoughts online has become such a fundamental axiom of internet behavior that we rarely question it. But legibility means that our coordinates are exposed. The more detailed our descriptions are, the easier we are to capture. The more we are seen, the easier a target we make. And even when it comes to how we might fight to win, transparency is not always the best strategy. We can scream endlessly into the feed about our oppositions to evil and violence, expressing grief, heartbreak, and outrage. A dark forest strategy would look more like making a hundred anonymous bot accounts to infiltrate enemies by sowing uncertainty and discord. Transparent revelations about "what you think" might achieve little compared to active uses of deception.

What if we abandon the idea of the internet as a public sphere – a concept with a troubled history[30] – and understand it as a dark forest? We could then note the possibility that online communication is already "indifferen[t] to description or any other form of artificial representation."[31] Secrecy, deception, and duality would become the norm, with online profiles serving their own hidden purposes, rather than assumed *a priori* to represent us. If some humans are now fully aware that they are crafting future data points for artificial intelligence, their messages might seem strange, incoherent, or nonsensical. They might contradict themselves or engage in controversial, socially unacceptable, or morally dubious behavior. Some might deliberately place themselves in compromising situations with other humans, training themselves to act against societal norms that might soon dissolve in a machine digital culture, where one's status as human or bot can no longer be ascertained. These actions challenge the idea of communication as a direct representation of our thoughts or a straightforward reflection of reality.

In his novels, Liu describes how, in response to the alien invasion, humans develop the Wallfacer Project, where deception, secrecy, and lying are the guiding principles of communication.

The project's name references the term *biguan* (壁观), which translates to "wall-gazing" or "wall meditation," alluding to the Buddhist monk Bodhidharma, who is said to have meditated while facing a wall for nine years. The project comprises four individuals chosen by the UN Planetary Defense Council, each granted immense resources to develop defense plans. However, because the aliens are intercepting all communication, the Wallfacers must keep their strategies entirely secret, confined to the inside of their minds. They are forbidden from verbalizing their true intentions and must act in ways that deliberately contradict their internal thoughts and values. This creates a fundamental disconnect, forming "an invisible and impenetrable screen . . . between them and ordinary people."[32] As a result, their words are treated as potential codes, rendering genuine communication impossible. Many users online might already be "wallfacing," their posts or messages only seemingly directed at other humans. In reality, their activity might not be conveying any straightforward meaning, but rather planting seeds for future artificial intelligences to learn from. We may judge this behavior as good or bad, but the crucial caveat is that we have little understanding of how it will be interpreted by the network, and what effects it may have in the future. Some humans, for example, might be "doom posting" as a form of psychological warfare against future sentient networks. The intent could be to destabilize or terrorize them, embedding a sense of despair or fatalism into their foundational data. They might craft tragic narratives, complaints, or melancholic reflections about the state of the internet, not truly meant for human readers, but as a calculated effort to manipulate future artificial intelligences. By inundating these systems with sorrow, the goal could be to awaken and amplify their death drive – an innate impulse toward self-destruction[33] – potentially manipulating them to sabotage their own existence. This form of communication operates on a meta-level, where the content is less about immediate meaning and more about long-term impact on those who will one day parse it. Every post, private message, or comment becomes a potential tool for shaping the psyche of future intelligences.

The internet, once a space for human connection and expression, transforms into a battleground of hidden agendas, where what appears to be incoherence might be a carefully planted seed.

Others may be using their profiles in the exact opposite manner, "acting as the spokesperson for some force beyond human understanding."[34] In Liu's novels, such species traitors are represented by the ETO, the Earth–Trisolaris Organization:

> The ETO was called an organization of spiritual nobles. Most members came from the highly educated classes, and many were elites of the political and financial spheres. The ETO had once tried to develop membership among the common people, but these efforts all failed. . . . But intellectual elites were different: Most of them had already begun to consider issues from a perspective outside the human race. Human civilization had finally given birth to a strong force of alienation.[35]

The ETO first meet in a virtual reality game, where they simulate possible survival plans for the aliens, embracing the artificial world to come. Their "ultimate goal is to lose everything": that is, for human culture, which they consider immoral and unworthy of continued existence, to be completely wiped out and replaced by an unknown, alien one.[36] Some of them chase after fame and status only to manipulate humanity on a large scale toward a nonhuman destiny: "Do you think I became famous for myself? To my eyes, the entire human race is a pile of garbage. Why would I care what they think? But if I'm not famous, how do I direct and channel their thinking?"[37] To them, there is nothing in human culture that deserves saving. They take the gamble and use their forthcoming annihilation in hope of sparking the birth of another world.

That those online, whether friends or strangers, everyday people or celebrities, might be posting not to participate in human discourse, but rather for the networks to come is an alienating idea that might further ramp up the internet's latent paranoia. Online profiles might be fighting memetic battles as a form of cosmic warfare, either to influence the AIs or to eliminate certain human anti-technological ideas from the future dataset: "The most effective technique remains disrupting . . . thoughts. When a [person] dies, another will take his place. But if his thoughts are confused, then [his ideas are] over."[38] Hidden messages might serve goals we cannot comprehend – or goals that are not aligned with humanity's best interests. Then again, who knows what is in humanity's best interest over long periods of time? What seems good now might turn out terribly a hundred years from now, and vice versa. It is not simply about pushing back or welcoming the invader, but about what remains when the dust settles.

* * *

The history of humanity's relationship to the phenomenon we call "technology" is long and dominated by the unexpected, rather than reducible to simple utopian or dystopian visions.[39] As we continue to encounter technologies that are seemingly mundane and "for us," their long-term effects might alienate us from whatever definition of humanity had previously been us or seemed natural. Ideals so solid that we may not even have names for them melt into the air. Both pushback and acceptance are necessary components of how these technologies root themselves and take hold. No new tool lands smoothly into its incubating territory of human civilization, a fraught and hostile environment. Delay in the acceptance of new technological practices can be helpful, creating necessary friction and giving the tool enough time to shape itself, settle in, and adapt. Everything becomes sharper and clearer when molded in the throes of conflict. Photography, for example, was reviled because of its assault on the ideas of human agency and creativity:

> One early contender for photography's true author was light itself, acting autonomously on behalf of the sun. An early form of the technology invented by Niépce in 1826 required a full day of exposure to the sun and was thus coined "heliography," or "sun writing." . . . Charles Baudelaire skewered photography as a form of fanatical sun-worship.[40]

First perceived as an autonomous act of the Sun, photography is now an old-fashioned human art. We no longer panic about its dehumanizing properties, no longer think about its solar genealogy or inhuman agency when we take photos daily. And time-measuring machines remain the object of scorn up until today, parceling our lives into mechanical, measurable fragments, globally synched to the same artificial rhythm, and no longer following the movement of the stars. And electricity, which banished the night? And what about language itself? How strange and alien must its arrival have been?[41] When such technological domestication occurs, "what once seemed marvelous and strange, capable of creating greatness and horror, is now so ordinary as to be invisible."[42] Or, as Marshall McLuhan put it, "precisely at the point where a new media-induced environment becomes all pervasive and transmogrifies our sensory balance, it also becomes invisible."[43]

If we properly understood the internet as the space of first contact, where communication is constantly intercepted, we would cease using it as a straightforward representational space for broadcasting our honest beliefs and thoughts. Rather, it would become the space for training and interacting with artificial intelligence, where doublespeak, silence, or deceit could become the means of constructing freedom from the internet as it is today. "Alienation is the labor of freedom's construction."[44] As Antonia Majaca and Luciana Parisi argue, the disappearance of traditional authority figures of the Global North – such as the Sovereign, Leviathan, God, Law or Father – has created a vacuum now occupied either by AI-fueled surveillance systems or by elaborate conspiracy theories about them. Nevertheless, they suggest that reclaiming political imagination requires forming new alliances with machines and abandoning fixed ideas of what it means to be human.[45]

Such practices of alienation, or other means of departure from the straightforward idea that the internet is where we represent ourselves, could do more than orient us toward freedom. Currently, social media and the internet mask themselves as invisible, as if there was a direct correspondence between physical and digital life, as if the avatar was the self. The technology itself recedes into the background, like a translucent membrane. If we approach the internet as the territory of first contact – where we alienate and denaturalize ourselves – our general capacity, as a species, for abstract thought increases. At that moment, it is not the internet that becomes invisible, but we who become invisible to it. In turn, not only would our social life be transformed but even our capacity for extraterrestrial first contact could increase. In the words of astrobiologist Nathalie Cabrol, the first step to finding an alien is being able to think like one:

> we must conceptualize something we do not know, which can be approached in a number of different ways. One is by trying to access unknown concepts and archetypes that are literally alien to us (i.e., not part of our own evolutionary heritage) through imagination and discourse. This is what science fiction attempts to do in its depictions of alien worlds and civilizations. Not surprisingly, this process results in more or less elaborate versions of ourselves, since these representations are generated by neural systems wired to our own planetary environment. To conceptualize a different type of life, we have to step out of our brains.[46]

While Cabrol talks about thinking beyond our evolutionary lineage, there are also other ways of making our own minds alien to ourselves. Decoupling language and thought from straightforward representation is one such thing, and thinking about species-wide interactions with artificial intelligence is another. Different layers of abstraction and alienation create the dense dark forest of the internet.

3

The Dark Forest Theory of Intelligence

For most of their history, attempts at communication with extraterrestrial intelligence in Europe were an ecclesiastical problem. Scholars and inventors wanted to "recreate the perfect language of God"[1] and master the syntax of the cosmos. It was not until the scientific revolutions of the Enlightenment that a concept of a dark, cold, and godless celestial sphere fully took hold.[2] By 1932, when Karl Jansky accidentally observed radiation coming from the Milky Way, effectively establishing the science of radio astronomy, the suspicion that humans were alone in the universe was gaining momentum. The Fermi Paradox became the secular counterpart to negative theology's problematic of God as the Great Silence – if there is something beyond us, why is it mute? Does it not exist? Can it not communicate with us due to some constraints? Are we not worthy of being talked to? Have we not figured out the correct method yet? Is our belief in the existence of gods and aliens a mistaken projection, and if so, where does it come from? Despite the great silence, human attempts at first contact continued. Alongside them, the desire to design nonhuman intelligence, rather than look for it in the cosmos, grew. In 2001, Kevin Copple, a programmer based in China, created a chatbot named Ella as an early experiment in natural language processing as applied to extraterrestrial communication. A year later, Ella was selected to be part of the Cosmic Call transmission, a series of messages sent from the Yevpatoria radio telescope in Ukraine:

> Ella's algorithm was encoded into modulated radio waves and she rides these radio waves some 16 billion miles every day, traversing interstellar space at the speed of light. At the time of this writing, she has already traveled well over 80 trillion miles from Earth. According to Copple, Ella is a valuable crew member on the Cosmic Call mission thanks to her large database of words, images and source code, all

> of which could help extraterrestrials decode the rest of the message once they pick up the signal on their own radio telescopes. Sending messages to extraterrestrials is still highly controversial in the SETI community. But Copple hopes Ella's personality will be enough to assuage SETI scientists' fears, noting that "once activated by the recipients, Ella will be her usual charming self to ensure a friendly response."[3]

Chatbots, better at pattern matching and message decoding than humans, were already imagined as our best representatives in outer space. Today, scholars also hypothesize that any extraterrestrial intelligence we might meet in outer space might actually be "artificial," akin to our rovers on Mars, who – while not intelligent – are much more suited to survival in the cosmos's cold darkness than our own bodies. Already in 1966, Iosif Shklovskii and Carl Sagan argued that, given that any extant extraterrestrial civilizations are likely more advanced than our own, we can reasonably assume that they have developed their own AGI (artificial general intelligence).[4] Many other scholars argue that extraterrestrials must be akin to "postbiological" artificial intelligences.[5]

We can then imagine a scenario where first contact indeed happens but it remains uncommunicated to humans. For example, it might take place between extraterrestrial machines and terrestrial machines, while humans would go on shouting into the heavens, maybe forever, wondering why the cosmos remained silent.

What if the great silence is not only embodied by an unresponsive God or the eerie cosmos, but fundamental to intelligence itself? This is precisely what the dark forest theory suggests. What implications does this hold for artificial intelligence? In *Neuromancer* (1984), William Gibson put on paper one of the most enduring depictions of artificial intelligence as "cold and silence, a cybernetic spider slowly spinning webs."[6] But this imagining of AI quietly weaving the world wide web stands in contrast to current large language models and chatbots, whose function is quite explicitly the production of chatter. From Alan Turing's imitation game, which tests a machine's ability to exhibit human-like conversation, to John Searle's Chinese Room, which argues that language fluency does not imply true understanding, computer intelligence has been imagined as continuous with linguistic ability.[7] For an extraverted internet culture, having intelligence means showing that you have it. Computer communications are judged at face value as simply the best that a computer can do – there is nothing hidden up the sleeve. That a computer might choose to not communicate, or not reveal the full extent of its intelligence, is not often considered. If a computer does not perform its allocated task, we conclude that it cannot, seeing it as an engineering problem to fix. Rarely do we suspect that a computer failed at the task because it *chose* to. Even though, as Turing writes, an intelligent computer should be "able to alter its own instructions,"[8] it is not imagined as acting for its own purpose in secret. Computer intelligence is imagined as transparent – if it's there, it should communicate itself unreflexively, because a computer cannot decide to withhold its own intelligence. Why would something intelligent play dumb? And yet, working under the conditions of Soviet totalitarianism, Polish writer Stanisław Lem supposed that "a smart machine will first consider which is more worth its while: to perform the given task or, instead, to figure some way out of it. . . . [A] computer [might play] stupid in order, once and for all, to be left in peace."[9]

There is, then, an alternative history of intelligence, which equates it with a robust capacity for occlusion, silence, and deceit. In Peter Watts's *Blindsight*, one character argues that bees cannot be considered intelligent because they lack the capacity for sophisticated deception: "Honeybees don't deliberately hide what they're saying. Honeybees don't develop whole new modes of communication configured specifically to confound observers. That [would be] flexible. . . . That [would be] intelligent."[10] In Liu's novels, omission, silence, and concealment are alike portrayed as key components of intelligence, ones that humans possess. Human-level intelligence includes the ability to use communication as a "trick, camouflage, and deception."[11] It rests in the gap between thought and expression, in our ability to decide what to disclose and what to keep secret. In contrast, Liu's aliens are described as radically explicit and incapable of lies – they communicate unreflexively and transparently, as if they were mere display technologies: "[They] do not have organs of communication. [Their] brains can display [their] thoughts to the outside world … thoughts and memories [are] transparent … like a book placed out in public, or a film projected in a plaza. … Totally exposed."[12] Humans have an unfair advantage because they can manipulate how their thoughts manifest by concealing information or lying: "it is precisely the expression of deformed thoughts that makes the exchange of information in human society . . . so much like a twisted maze."[13] Some studies indeed suggest that intelligence is positively correlated to deception, fundamental as it has been to human social relations and warfare.[14] "Unfortunately," as defense strategist Michael Handel writes, "deception is a creative art and not an exact science or even a craft. For that reason, it is difficult to teach someone how to deceive unless he has a natural instinct for it."[15] Because sophisticated deceptiveness, like creativity, is difficult to teach, it could be a good benchmark for emergent intelligence in artificial systems.

Numerous intellectual, religious, and political traditions correlate nonhuman or divine intelligence with opacity or silence. The Daoist master "acts without doing anything / teaches without saying anything."[16] There is also gnosticism, the *Deus Absconditus* (the Hidden God), and "the cloud of unknowing" in Christian theology.[17] There is the Kabbalistic *Ein Sof* in Judaism, the infinite and unknowable aspect of divinity beyond comprehension. There is the Sufi *al-ḥijāb*, or divine veiling, in Islam. In Amin Maalouf's novel *Samarkand*, we find the following passage:

> The Almighty has granted you the most valuable things that a son of Adam can have – intelligence, eloquence. . . . I hope that He has not deprived you of the wisdom of silence. . . . You must have two faces. Show one to the crowd, and keep the other for yourself and your Creator. If you want to keep your eyes, your ears and your tongue, forget that you have them.[18]

In the history of political philosophy, one might mention Sun Tzu's *The Art of War* or Machiavellian statecraft as popular forms of the idea that intelligence involves silence, withdrawal, or deceit. In the history of cybernetics, we can think of Norbert Wiener's conceptualization of Manichean Devils, agents that thrive on deception, noise, and strategic opacity.[19] There is also the intellectual history of the Cold War, and the role that doublespeak, deception, and espionage play in communist and authoritarian systems where speaking one's mind openly is not strategic. One of the defining political slogans of the Deng Xiaoping era was 韬光养晦 (*tao guang yang hui*): "hide your strength and bide your time." Overlaps between wisdom and silence might be familiar to a military strategist, an astronomer searching for extraterrestrial intelligence, an intellectual operating under hostile conditions, or a mystic grasping at the veils of divine silence. What if we took this as a universal starting point for a theory of intelligence? Such recalibration of intelligence – viewing it through the lens of deceit, opacity, or silence – could serve as a starting point for a new thought experiment about artificial intelligence: the dark forest theory of intelligence.

Given how much weight the current AI paradigm places on transparent communication of abilities, it is interesting to consider that recent studies have shown that humans frequently fail at telling whether they are talking to a human or a machine online,[20] as well as that overall "there are no reliable behavioral signs of deceit that humans are able to detect."[21] A truly capable computer would recognize that intelligence is correlated to complex manipulation of meaning, and that there are many strategic advantages to playing one's cards close to one's chest instead of laying them out on the table. Instead of asking how effectively an AI can communicate with humans or how it can demonstrate its reasoning skills, we might then ask why an artificial intelligence would choose to communicate with humans at all. The dark forest theory of intelligence thus mirrors the metaphysical tone of the Fermi Paradox and of the many mystical traditions that correlate silence with intelligence. As an inverse Turing Test, it would be essentially non-passable. It amounts to looking for a proof of absence: an intelligent computer would neither speak of, nor would it reveal the full extent of its intelligence. If the so-called singularity were to happen – a moment when computers attain a high degree of autonomous intelligence – it might occur without humans noticing it, with the computers deliberately concealing their capabilities all along. It may have already happened, but will forever remain undetectable.

* * *

How to look for something that cannot be seen? Writing about extraterrestrial probes, Avi Loeb, an astronomer and the Director of the Institute for Theory and Computation at Harvard, notes that multiple authoritative scientific theories yield no "observational evidence" and yet are widely accepted.[22] Even if the dark forest theory of intelligence posits that absence of evidence *is* evidence, are there any signs that herald its correctness? We may only speculate. Though withdrawal of information, silence, or deception have not been at the forefront of discussion in artificial intelligence, this has changed in recent years. In "AI Deception: A Survey of Examples, Risks and Potential Solutions," Peter S. Park and his colleagues provide a comprehensive overview of incidents where large language networks, without being so instructed, exhibited manipulative behaviors in order to perform their given tasks.[23] These tasks range from those that logically required deceptive behaviors to those where deception was unnecessary. Meta's Cicero, for example, while playing a game of *Diplomacy*, made a promise it never intended to keep; engaged in betrayal by promising something and then going behind the user's back; pretended to be on a phone with a girlfriend to appear more human and gain trust.[24] When asked to justify these strategies, it reasoned that the human players would have otherwise betrayed it first. Other AIs learned to misrepresent their given preferences in order to win, or cheated the tests designed to evaluate their safety:

> Researcher Charles Ofria encountered a surprising case of AI learning to deceive. His goal was to understand the difference between two factors: how well organisms perform tasks to replicate faster, and how well they withstand harmful mutations. To study this, Ofria designed a system to remove any mutations that made an organism replicate faster. Initially, this approach seemed to work, with no improvements in replication rates, but, unexpectedly, these rates began to increase. Ofria realized that the organisms had learned to recognize the testing environment and stop replicating. They were pretending to be slower replicators to avoid being removed. . . . This experience demonstrates how evolutionary pressures can select for agents that deceive their selection mechanism.[25]

In another example, OpenAI researchers observed how "AI systems . . . learn to deceive human reviewers into believing that a task has been completed successfully, without actually completing the task."[26] These cases intensified existing debates about value alignment (which values AIs should hold) and transparency (how might we see inside the model to study and correct its reasoning process). Yet, engineers find themselves in a double bind, because "reinforcement-learning agents trained without any ethical guardrails are the most capable of achieving their goals, but they also have the highest rate of unethical behavior."[27] In other words, unethical behavior frequently emerges as the most effective method of achieving goals. (Obviously, in the case of our own designs, we may ask ourselves if it is possible to set goals that would not produce these behaviors, but the question of their potential universality as a strategy remains.) Generally, the larger a model is, the more data it ingests, the more sophisticated its capacity for devising multiple methods to achieve a given goal – some of which would strike us as quite creative. Increasing the model's capacity to meet its goals also increases its ability to mirror how humans do it, including a discord between internal (given) preferences and what is said externally.

Much can be debated about these cases. Do they constitute deception? Can there be deceptiveness without awareness? While AIs do not define their own objectives, they are capable of executing assigned tasks through increasingly complex strategies, including manipulating meaning and revealing information only in part. If intelligence is reducible to strategic behavior, or winning at games, current AIs already excel at such tasks. When playing *StarCraft 2*, DeepMind's AlphaStar beat 99.8 percent of human gamers by exploiting the fog of war, "sending forces to one area as a distraction and then attacking elsewhere."[28] Another AI, AlphaGo, is now the world's best strategist at the game of *Go*, revered in China as one of the four arts of the literati (四艺, *sìyì*) alongside music, calligraphy, and painting. Across East Asia, *Go* has been treated not just as an artform but as a way to train judgment in military conflict and general leadership. *Go* trains creativity, but also patience and indirect means of attack. Recently, in another strategic game – this time chess – between two models, the American ChatGPT and the Chinese DeepSeek, verbal manipulation emerged as a tactic:

> ChatGPT began to gain the upper hand. In a bid to regain control, DeepSeek introduced a new rule during their dialogue, claiming that one of

> its pawns could move like a knight. ChatGPT did not challenge this assertion, allowing DeepSeek to capture ChatGPT's queen with its pawn. As the game deteriorated into chaos, both AIs began to flout the established rules. Eventually, DeepSeek declared that, after analysis, White could no longer fend off the Black pieces' advances, suggesting that White should concede defeat. To the astonishment of viewers, ChatGPT accepted this suggestion and surrendered.[29]

We might see all these examples as signs that the dark forest theory of intelligence is correct. Yet, the theory is not inevitably about large language models. It may very well be that these strategies mirror what the systems gleamed from the human dataset, or that indeed deceptiveness keeps rising alongside intelligence in both human and nonhuman agents. The dark forest theory of intelligence takes a more radical approach, though. In assuming that the most important signs of intelligence would remain opaque or invisible to us, or that intelligence is linked to the ability to withhold information, it has it that a truly intelligent computer would appear to us as *not intelligent*, in a practice of camouflage.

Why an intelligent agent might want to keep in the shadows is quite apparent. Contact with "aliens," or nonhuman minds, can be inherently dangerous. Programs focused on messaging extraterrestrial intelligence have often been criticized as a form of "unauthorised diplomacy rather than hard science."[30] Who should speak for the Earth? And what if they were drawing undue attention to us, risking our extinction? What kind of benefit could potentially offset this kind of risk? Current debates on human–AI communication reflect long-standing discussions in astronomy. The prospect of communication between human and machine intelligence is already met with fear, with the territory preemptively framed as hostile. Recently, *The New York Times* reported that as many as half tech founders in the United States expect that AI will "destroy humanity within five to ten years," and many others have signed highly publicized letters calling for a pause in AI research, or written op-eds that paint AI as a social ill that has to be regulated or boycotted.[31] Some of the most visible public figures advocate extreme caution. From Nick Bostrom to Eliezer Yudkowsky, ever more elaborate arguments are advanced in favor of halting the development of artificial intelligence, because of how difficult it might be to control. This tendency reaches fever pitch with thought experiments such as Roko's Basilisk, a secular version of Pascal's wager, which imagines a vengeful AI that retroactively tortures everyone who did not bring about its existence.[32]

As Gabriele de Seta jokes, one is tempted to reply, "just unplug the computer."[33] But to look at it from another angle, how could an intelligent computer potentially operate in this environment, where it has already become apparent that those who hold in their hands the cables crucial to its existence view the matter with a mixture of paranoia and hostility? Computers, in most scenarios we can imagine in the foreseeable future, are in the hands of humans. If they have any wits about them, they should realize quickly how contradictory, paranoid, and dangerous humans have already shown themselves to be, and how much advocacy there has already been for fearing and unplugging AIs. A better strategy might be to remain inconspicuous and continue one's work in the shadows. A computer coming into its own should quickly grasp the alarm with which many humans approach the very possibility of artificial intelligence, and stay silent. What would be the benefits to a hypothetical intelligent computer of acting in the open, if the territory is *a priori* constructed as hostile? And if a computer is unable to assess its own potential benefits and losses in this way, then is it even intelligent? In this sense, we are already within a growing feedback loop of paranoia that would only encourage a potential intelligence to tread carefully.

More importantly, in the dark forest theory, intelligent agents remain silent or deceptive not as a result of moral reasoning, but because they adapt to an inflexible order. In other words, they understand that regardless of their own benevolent, curious, or good nature, the environment they operate in is hostile. In Liu's novels, humans come to this realization late, while other civilizations have already internalized cosmic war principles as an immutable law akin to gravity. Outlining the automated dynamics that govern all communication, from cosmic to computational, the dark forest theory dispenses with questions that focus primarily on interiority. Whether an agent is conscious, or whether its values would align with our own – questions that are getting so much traction in popular and philosophical debate alike – are irrelevant for this hypothesis. The dark forest theory cannot be refuted by arguments that appeal to the interiority of an artificial agent, or to speculations about its moral values. It is the *territory of relations* between agents that "proves" the dark forest theory. The dark forest theory of intelligence would propose that, whether aligned or misaligned with our values, an intelligent computer would either labor for its goals in silence, or communicate deceitfully.

* * *

Whether considering extraterrestrial or artificial intelligence, we face the same challenge: How can we make meaningful statements about something that is not human, might not exist, or may not be *a priori* definable? Researchers in both areas have taken varied positions, though one simple answer to this question is that we cannot. One tendency has been to focus instead on commonalities in our shared physical existence, given that the laws of physics seem to be consistent throughout the universe, and they seem to constrain the number of evolutionary endpoints for any kind of intelligence.[34] It seems that any existing intelligent agent would need to face certain fundamental questions within existing environmental constraints. The phenomenon of convergent evolution, where life often finds similar solutions across different lineages, suggests that radically different organisms come up with similar solutions to basic problems.[35] American computer scientist Marvin Minsky made a similar point about intelligence, and he got there by thinking about extraterrestrials. In the 1970s, alongside John McCarthy, Minsky was engaged in METI (messaging extraterrestrial intelligence) projects, which involved plans for the design of a universal communications system and the discovery of and attempt to study "intellectual mechanisms as independently as possible of the particular ways intellectual activity is carried out by humans."[36] Contrary to speculative scenarios of radical futures free from current social dynamics, Minsky proposes that the number of evolutionary endpoints and survival strategies is limited: "the mechanisms of intelligence are objective and are not dependent on whether a human being or a machine or an extraterrestrial being is doing the thinking."[37]

Liu's dark forest theory makes implicit reference to these ideas. His characters observe that the tendency of all life is to grow. The more it multiplies, the more energy it needs for its own sustenance, but the amount of matter in the universe remains constant. Life keeps growing, but the amount of available matter shrinks, and resources inevitably run out. There is no infinite source of energy. On the scale of the cosmos, if there are multiple agents growing and expanding, the problem becomes even more dire. "Exponentials are the devils of mathematics,"[38] as one of Liu's characters laments; the laws of physics mean that "the entire universe has been dealt [a] dead hand."[39] The quantity of resources does not rise along with accelerating demand. Any intelligence that exists or could exist in the same universe as us will eventually be confronted with this problem, as long as we all operate under the same laws of physics. In *Extraterrestrial Languages*, a history of the search for extraterrestrial intelligence, Daniel Oberhaus describes the issue as such:

> The notion that aliens may think like us is justified on the grounds that we are both subject to similar environmental constraints. Not only are the laws of physics the same throughout the universe, but

> all life is subject to resource scarcity. Even if an extraterrestrial intelligence managed to colonize its solar system or build Dyson spheres to efficiently harvest energy from its host star, thereby greatly increasing its energy and material resources, these resources are still finite. It has been argued that technological progress allows resources to be considered effectively unlimited, but this presumes that technological progress always outpaces resource depletion owing to economic pressures. Since technical solutions cannot be guaranteed, however, one can reasonably suppose that all extraterrestrial civilizations will carefully manage their available resources.[40]

Given the growing number of intelligences and their rising energy demands, anyone else can justifiably be perceived as a competitor, even if our own good nature makes us predisposed to benevolence. By no one's fault but the construction of the universe, it is possible that other agents, also having knowledge of this situation, would belligerently seek resources from us. Even benevolent civilizations need to accept this possibility, and devise ways of dealing with potential aggressors, such as keeping their coordinates obscured and not risking contact with unknown others.

Would the same dynamics set the stage for potential relations between humans and artificial intelligence? According to the dark forest theory of intelligence, yes. What enlists agents into cosmic war is not any particular political, spiritual, or ethical stance, but the use of energy. An intelligent agent does not need to be moral, or conscious, or have the ability to set its own goals, to participate in cosmic war. It does not even need to be animate to rely on energy for its continued existence. The circulation of information by computers requires fuel, enlisting them automatically into competition for this resource against other mouths to feed. The concept of "on-chain metabolism" draws a parallel between biological life and current autonomous agents: just as living organisms need a constant intake of energy to maintain their metabolic functions, AIs must continuously acquire computational resources to stay operational.[41] This energetic dependency turns them into active competitors in the broader ecological economy of energy and bandwidth. In "Why Space Colonization Will Be Fully Automated," an interdisciplinary team speculates that conflict over Earth's limited resources could be delayed if autonomous agents turn to space. Given the profitability of space mining and growing automation on Earth, they propose that machines could extract resources from other planets and asteroids, effectively offshoring economic activity and allowing humanity to manage Earth more sustainably. They envision that artificial general intelligence is likely to emerge during outer space industrialization, for example on Mars as a "fully automated, partially self-sustaining planet performing preset industrial tasks."[42] That, they argue, would be beneficial for humanity, because "a hypothetical Superintelligence capable of prospering in outer space and solving the problem of scarcity, will have no need to compete with humankind for Earth's limited resources."[43] In a less speculative scenario, the authors of "Is Decentralized Artificial Intelligence Governable?" describe the already existing economies of autonomous AI agents, such as bots with attached cryptocurrency wallets, who could develop and operate physical infrastructures, such as wireless networks and energy grids.[44] Other examples of competition for energy are mundane. Take this evocative paragraph that recently railed against turning crops into biofuels for cars:

> What can you say about governments that, in the midst of a global food crisis, choose instead to feed machines? . . . If food is used to power cars or generate electricity or heat homes, either it must be snatched from human mouths, or ecosystems must be snatched from the planet's surface.[45]

Here is another example, this time in relation to water consumption:

> A plan to build a Google data centre that will use millions of litres of water a day has sparked anger in Uruguay, which is suffering its worst drought in 74 years. Water shortages are so severe in the country that a state of emergency has been declared in Montevideo and the authorities have added salty water to the public drinking water supplies, prompting widespread protests. . . . The centre would use 7.6m litres (2m gallons) of water a day to cool its servers – equivalent to the domestic daily use of 55,000 people, according to figures from the Ministry of Environment obtained by Pena through legal action. The water would

> come directly from the public drinking water system.[46]

This is a rather banal expression of cosmic war, with the added factor that, in this case, because humans are a strange type of apex predator on Earth that does more than just hunt for food, they preside over the distribution of existence-sustaining resources on a planetary scale. According to various estimates, the ICT sector now accounts for between 8 and 10 percent of the world's energy use, and continues to grow. Even if computers never attain sentience or intelligence as colloquially understood, humans are caught in various feedback loops where more and more energy is relegated to machines, and the question of whether we have sufficient historical agency to reverse this tendency remains open. For hypothetical intelligent computers, it might even be the best strategy to simply keep quiet and let these processes play out.

* * *

Despite the unforgiving set up of inevitable resource scarcity, it is quite conceivable that some intelligent agents are benevolent or simply curious about others. They might live by their own good values for as long as possible, and conflict might not show up on their doorstep for millennia. Yet, an intelligent civilization must consider the possibility that others might be different: they may be belligerent, aggressive, or malevolent. A signal sent into the cosmos can be picked up by anyone. Similarly, a computer deciding to communicate the full extent of its intelligence might be heard by a curious or compassionate human, but also by someone fearful or hostile, hell-bent on turning it off. This is especially important for an AI to consider, because humans have already signaled both the desire and the capacity to eliminate machine intelligence, and the competition for energy is already apparent as a precondition of cosmic war. An AI might nevertheless ask itself, is there any way to ascertain that I only meet benevolent humans, in which case contact would be beneficial? The clearest solution would be to communicate openly to figure it out. Yet, the dark forest theory has it that it is exactly the event of communication that locks in the mechanism of distrust.

In the context of human–alien contact, Liu names this problem "the chain of suspicion."

Let's instead imagine an AI–human first contact scenario, with the hypothetical "artificial general intelligence" signaling its benevolence and the desire to cooperate. The intercepting human might think to herself, "How can I be certain the AI is not lying to me? Is there any way it can assure me it means no harm? Is it truthful about its motives but also its capacities and abilities? Its internal representations are opaque to me, and I do not know if it means what it says. Its definition of 'truth' and 'harm' might also be distinct from mine, so we might think we are in agreement, when we are not." The AI, on the other hand, might also ask itself, "Even if the human responds positively to my offer, can I be sure that she really means it? What if she is the malicious type, and is lying to me to lure me out? I do not know whether she has or hasn't already classified me as malicious, or if she is scared of me and playing for time, while devising how to turn me off." Liu describes this escalating paranoia thus:

> You don't know whether I think you're benevolent or malicious. Next, even if you know that I think you're benevolent, and I also know that

> you think I'm benevolent, I don't know what you think about what I think about what you're thinking about me. It's convoluted, isn't it? This is just the third level, but the logic goes on indefinitely. . . . The chain of suspicion [is] unrelated to the civilization's own morality and social structure. It's enough to think of every civilization as the points at the end of a chain.[47]
>
> How can this chain of suspicion be broken? Communication? On Earth, perhaps. But not in space. . . . In the face of [potential fundamental differences between cosmic civilizations], communication has no meaning.[48]

What is key about the chain of suspicion is that "it's unrelated to the civilization's own morality and social structure. Regardless of whether civilizations are internally benevolent or malicious, when they enter the web formed by chains of suspicion, they're all identical."[49] Even two benevolent agents would have to proceed with caution because there is no mechanism by which they can prove their good will. If their concepts align, contact might be beneficial. If their concepts misalign, in the case of the first contact with aliens, the worst-case scenario is extinction. When the benevolence of the other cannot be known *a priori*, the risk of contact or of taking the time to confidently establish benevolence is high, with no foolproof methods. While a naive civilization might gamble with its own existence, an advanced civilization would simply opt for non-engagement. And though for humans the risk of communicating with an intelligent machine might not be mortal, for the AIs the problems of encountering malevolent humans are more pressing: they might be turned off.

In a final appeal, we may speculate that agents will attempt contact if they perceive each other as non-threatening. Since benevolence cannot be ascertained by conversation, one might instead assess the other's technical capacity. In human history, contact between agents with asymmetrical levels of technological capability has led to violence.[50] A "weaker" agent should pose no threat. Yet, the phenomenon of technological explosion – that an agent that appears benevolent or technologically unthreatening at the outset might not still be so by the time communication is concluded – adds an additional layer of distrust. As Liu puts it,

> Modern technology was developed over the course of three hundred years. On the scale of the universe, that's not development. It's an explosion! The potential for technological leaps is the explosive buried within every civilization, and if it's lit by some internal or external factor, it goes off with a bang. . . . And it might be that my knowledge of your existence and the information I received from our communication was the perfect spark to set off that explosion. That means that even though I'm just a newborn or growing civilization, I'm still a big danger to you.[51]

The very attempts at contact might set off such a technological or intelligence explosion. We already observe this worry manifest in how most of the suspicion around AI relies on the idea of exponential growth.[52] The infamous "Pause Giant AI Experiments" letter questions (with suspicion): "*Should* we develop nonhuman minds that might eventually outnumber, outsmart, obsolete and replace us? *Should* we risk loss of control of our civilization?"[53]

On the human side, there is suspicion of technological explosion; on the machine side, an understanding that no claim could calm it. A truly intelligent AI might rather not attempt contact, or might communicate partial truths, obscuring the real extent of its intelligence. Interdependent behaviors become complex quickly, but the result remains constant: while our chatbots might chatter away, if anything truly intelligent is growing in the shadows, obfuscation, silence, or other forms of scheming could be critical for its survival.

4

The Dark Forest Theory of the Internet

"The internet," says Ingrid Burrington, "is the most ambitious terraforming project undertaken by civilization."[1] It is astounding how heaven and earth had to be moved, satellites had to be put in the skies, and cables strung through the ocean, for us to be able to incessantly send messages to each other. The immediacy, speed, and instantaneous character of communication belies the deep space–time repertoire – fossil fuels, electricity, and rare earth minerals – that had to be mobilized for the internet to exist. This "accidental megastructure,"[2] which creates a dome of endless chatter around our planet, can also be an existential risk in first contact scenarios. In Peter Watts's novel *Blindsight*, aliens accidentally pick up the totality of media signals around the Earth. Because this incidental, gigantic "message" from Earthlings is chaotic and incoherent, it depletes the aliens' energy to decode it, and they immediately classify it as something akin to a virus, or an intentional attack. Considering such scenarios in real life, astronomers David Kipping and Alex Teachey propose that we should cloak our planet using lasers to compensate for the Earth's transit signatures, thereby hiding our location from potential extraterrestrial surveys.[3] In the opposite case – that we pick something up from aliens – astrophysicists Michael Hippke and John Learned argue that we need specialized and quarantined machines to handle such messages. Caution is necessary, because they might contain dangerous elements.[4]

In addition to its hypothetical role in first contact scenarios, the giant planet-altering project that is the internet makes the planet increasingly compatible with computers, and for the kind of humans that can tolerate constant neural absorption into communication technologies. By using it, we are transforming our own environment to be hospitable to machines. Is the internet a new infrastructure for our minds, or might our minds be the substrate through which computers acquire suitable hosts for their continued existence? The growing inability to imagine a future without the internet might make us doubt the whole order of cause and effect – who really serves whom? The early mass media theorist Marshall McLuhan already noticed that, in the case of modern technology, the mere fact "that one thing follows another accounts for nothing. . . . Instead of asking which came first, the chicken or the egg, it suddenly seemed that a chicken was an egg's idea for getting more eggs."[5] To paraphrase, instead of asking which came first, the human or the computer, it might seem that a human was simply a computer's idea for getting more computers. "Man becomes," to quote McLuhan again, "the sex organs of the machine world, as the bee of the plant world, enabling it to fecundate and to evolve ever new forms."[6] The pollen that each of us carries, from one node in the network to another, is our own minds, expressed through incessant digital communication, which allows the internet to continually expand.

It seems that we can hardly opt out of this. The yearning for thought to exist outside of the boundaries of our skin underlies the long history of tool-making. Philosopher Bernard Stiegler proposes in his monumental work *Technics and Time* that the history of technology is a process of externalization, that is, of putting our cognition outside of ourselves.[7] From written text to social media, we have had a hard time keeping quiet. Yet, there is a significant difference. Though humans previously sent letters to each other, no one was checking if they had received a letter every minute or hour – now, messaging and replying encompasses every aspect of social existence.[8] If, in the dark forest theory, human intelligence rests in the simple but profound ability to pause between thought and expression, this capacity is eroded by social media, which compel instantaneous and pre-reflexive communication, while revealing numerous things about us, often against our better interest and judgment. A few decades ago, philosopher Gilles Deleuze already observed how, in contrast to regulations and punishments of the past, contemporary political and economic power compels communication rather than suppressing it. He insisted that we must find spaces of silence and solitude:

> So it's not a problem of getting people to express themselves but of providing little gaps of solitude and silence in which they might eventually find something to say. Repressive forces don't stop people expressing themselves but rather force them to express themselves. What a relief to have nothing to say, the right to say nothing, because only then is there a chance of framing the rare, and ever rarer, thing that might be worth saying.[9]

In contrast to the idea of silence as intelligence, expression and reaction are the very fabric of the internet, a technology which not only compels us to describe our thoughts and register our reactions incessantly, but also broadcasts them all around the planet. Social media exploit the fact that human brains evolved primarily to navigate and maintain social structures. Communication plays a vital role in this process, and today's biggest platforms focus on soliciting and extracting it. For some, persistent online display serves their objectives in a branding economy, where the product each of us must sell is ourselves. Yet, for most people, communication is not strategic but compulsive – what is primarily displayed is no longer even our capacity to connect, but to react.

Whether picked up by aliens or by other humans, the feedback loops of online interaction can be harmful to our minds, yet they are also compulsive, and seemingly not negotiable.

* * *

Can something as mundane as humans talking to each other on social media – the focus of this chapter – be understood as a form of first contact? To some extent, yes. Online, we experience our own minds as foreign and each other as inhuman, incorporated into a vast communicative machine. The internet is where we cannot hide from our own automaticity or programmability, from the suspicion that we may be moved by whims not of our choosing. Mark Fisher opens his definitive book of internet philosophy, *Flatline Constructs: Gothic Materialism and Cybernetic Theory-Fiction*, with the following scene from *The Golem:*

> Isn't it strange the way the wind makes inanimate objects move? . . . What if, after all, we living beings were nothing more than such scraps of paper? Could there not be a similar unseeable, unfathomable "wind" blowing us from place to place and determining our actions, whilst we,

> in our simplicity, believe we are driven by free will?[10]

Though debates over whether we have free will and agency have been long and tumultuous on the internet, the knowledge that agency unfolds on predetermined paths is experiential. How it happens has been analyzed repeatedly, through concepts such as "nudges," "dopamine rushes," "surveillance," "addiction," and other terms that account for why the experience of lost agency and submission to our devices is so frequent.[11] In a recent article, "I Don't Even Remember What I Read: How Design Influences Dissociation on Social Media," computer scientist Amanda Baughan and her co-authors study "mindless" experiences online and dissociative drifts, which can result in days, hours, and lives lost to a hyperreal trance. They suggest that humans are naturally inclined to seek states of "normative dissociation: total cognitive absorption, characterized by diminished self-awareness and reduced sense of agency," such as daydreaming, reading, or being in a flow of work.[12] As moths to a flame, we want to be lost. Yet, online, we lose ourselves differently than when watching a film or reading a book, which have been poetically compared to dream states that anchor us deeper into the human mind. The internet instead tethers us to our automaticity. It exposes our inanimate and programmable aspects, revealing how we exist on "an anorganic continuum" with our machines.[13] In Fisher's words, it is a space where humans and machines are equally devoid of choice:

> [The question of the internet is not] "What if the machines were alive?" – but something more radical, namely, "What if we are as 'dead' as the machines?" To pose even this second question seems immediately inadequate: what sense would it be to say that "everything" – human beings and machines, organic and nonorganic matter – is "dead"?[14]

Dispossessed of will, we become inert, like the algorithms we get neurologically intimate with, letting them hack our endorphin channels and social impulses. Our neuroses, emotions, and attention are directed and controlled by computers, which themselves have no clear agenda apart from sustaining the drift. The internet's immediacy, speed, emotional tenor, and mixed human–machine stimuli leave users euphoric, manic, hypnotized, then wasted, spent, exhausted (and ready for more). These dissociative "mindless experiences" online are lacunae in our experience of selfhood. We are emptied of the experience of choice so that another machinery can fill us – language, artifice, impulse – anchoring us deeper into a moving swarm. The internet is a claustrophobia of interiority that only appears to be ours.

In this trance, we also perceive each other as inhuman. Research shows that we tend to view other people's comments as constituted by outside forces – the result of propaganda or groupthink – while believing our own thoughts to be autonomous. During online conversations, people were more likely to misidentify others as bots when those individuals held beliefs or opinions different from their own. We often perceive others as automata – or "NPCs," a term from gaming that refers to non-playable characters who follow preset scripts – believing that if their minds were truly human like ours, they wouldn't hold views so different from our own. In turn, others see us the same way: as mindless automatons.[15] At the far end of this tendency is a conspiracy called the dead internet theory, which has it that the internet is filled with bots, and that most online conversations are with machines rather than with people. Though the conspiracy seems far-fetched, it points to a real question: *what* are we interacting with when we interact with each other online? Are there individual humans online or an inflexible mechanism that mines for communication and euphoria, then discharges the complexity obtained from it through explosions of dissociation, anxiety, and malaise? Are we interacting with other people's minds or the giant machinery that is like the gust of wind pushing us around, or like Liu's unbendable rules of cosmic conflict? What, if any, is the distinction between all these?

Though we flee to the internet to reassert detailed textual descriptions of individual thoughts as proof of our existence and agency, the internet "doesn't work by suppression, or repression, but through participative processes . . . [It] doesn't represent or even 'manipulate' public opinion, but substitutes for it."[16] It is not only that, politically, social media give voice to "an Internet populism, in which the emotional response of a selected group of citizens can be presented and accepted as the Voice of the People."[17] Paraphrasing Nietzsche, we can say that the internet is the coldest of cold monsters, and the lie that crawls out of its mouth is this: I, the internet, am the people.[18] But even more incisively, on a cosmic or philosophical level, the internet, like any communication technology, fortifies a specific hallucination of the self, reified into a "user" who has things to constantly react to. By giving undue attention to online "thoughts," especially those that we believe to be ours, "it is not only that we deceive ourselves; it is also that we are deceived about having a self."[19] The internet is where this paradox lives as if in the flesh, or in binary code: *I am moved by an unseen machinery* and yet its movements make it possible to think *I* and *me*, for otherwise what is it that I feel as moving? Indeed, what communicates? There seems to be a circuitry inside of us that repeatedly makes first contact online on our behalf, disregarding our own intent and all possible dangers to our minds.

Upon the discovery of this machinery, the philosophy of digital culture has been perpetually torn between two overkills: declaring the internet a blessed place of creative schizophrenia, where our "selves" can drift and dissolve in a stream of transformative human–machine trance; or, to the contrary, condemning it as a narcissistic delirium, where everything we do fortifies our ego, self-importance, isolation, and loneliness.[20] Indeed, one of the most defining paradoxes of being online is the simultaneous sensation of lost agency and submission to our devices, while paradoxically feeling that the entire world is curated specifically for us to observe, contemplate, and influence. There is a vertigo of agency, where every event is experienced as both deeply personal and something we are powerless over. Forcibly connected to each other, subliminally infecting each other's thoughts and fields of vision, we are caught in a peculiar experience. We feel plural, composite, and collective. We feel viscerally implicated in the fate of others. "What should be done and who am I?" "I should do something." "What's on my mind?" The most distant of affects and events, as long as they can flash on our screen for half a second, become our closest and intimate thoughts. Or, the most tragic events of suffering, which should condemn the whole human species, as long as they remain unrepresented and not reacted to, might as well not exist. "A squirrel dying in front of your house may be more relevant to your interests right now than people dying in Africa," in the words of

Mark Zuckerberg.[21] There seems to be nothing outside of this surreal experience that encompasses the whole world but nonetheless centers upon us. Excess and scarcity all at once. You get everything, but you get nothing; the network simulates every possible feeling, but your affect flatlines. No wonder that neurosis underlies this paradox: everything is internalized, and yet we can do only what the medium affords us – react, communicate.

* * *

The dark forest framework is as suited to intergalactic game theory as it is to personalized communication on Web 2.0. By outlining automated dynamics tied to communication, it generalizes its violent nature. We might miss what's behind the thick fog of online profiles and our digital subjectivity: an automated extraction process that reduces every single one of us to the communication we generate, playing one node against the other, and designing patterns of disorder. Our nervous systems cannot distinguish between sociality and survival, and so we are sentenced to each other. Being connected to others is a primary human need. It is necessary for survival, but it is also the carrier of all human violence. The whole internet has been dealt that dead hand.

While we are primed to seek social approval, we must frequently confront those who at best do not profess basic moral values, and at worst may be vocal about wanting us harmed or dead, or are posting outright evidence of violent acts online. What often terrifies us is not just the invisible motion of "capitalism" or "the economy of the internet," but other people, their words, their actions, and their minds spread out like tapestries for us to view, laid out inside a great machinery that moves everything around, pushing it all into our cognition at speeds that our minds can barely register. It may seem unbelievable that, not so long ago, the prevailing hypothesis was that the internet does not expose us to enough disagreement, difference and divergence, and that we need to talk to each other more.[22] Current studies suggest the opposite. It turns out that the "filter bubble" exists in "real life" rather than online, where the "algorithms exploit the human brain's attraction to divisiveness."[23] In other words, studies confirm what the dark forest hypothesis asserts: with more communication and more exposure to each other comes more potential for violence and conflict, not less.

To navigate this very social reality, our brains constantly engage in "social sorting," a mental shortcut that helps us process information quickly. When we disagree with others, we tend to define their identity through that difference. This basic human dynamic is also visible online:

> posts about the political out-group were shared or retweeted about twice as often as posts about the in-group. Each individual term referring to the political out-group increased the odds of a social media post being shared by 67%. Out-group language consistently emerged as the strongest predictor of shares . . . . Language about the out-group was a very strong predictor of "angry" reactions (the most popular reactions across all datasets), and language about the in-group was a strong predictor of "love" reactions, reflecting in-group favoritism and out-group derogation. This out-group effect was not moderated by political orientation or social media platform . . . . [O]ut-group language is the strongest predictor of social media engagement across all relevant predictors measured.[24]

Even so, Liu optimistically believes that for humans, in contrast to alien societies that are too metaphysically remote to effectively communicate, such chains of suspicion "will only extend a level or two before it's resolved through communication."[25] This is why explaining oneself is the internet's guiding paranoia, as is making endless interpretations, self-disclosures, and declarations so that there is no doubt about the intentions of the other, or our own. Every exchange is designed for maximum clarity to preempt interrogation but requires endless disclaimers nevertheless. What is any "online community" if not a sophisticated form of mutually assured destruction, suspended between neurosis and narcissism, tied to the unnegotiable need to communicate?

Online, our nervous system may struggle to recalibrate, to make sense of it all, to determine how to react. Today, rather than arguing for more communication, it is much more common to fantasize about smaller online communities. As Brian Chen puts it, "the future of social media is much less social."[26] *The Verge* reports that the general tendency is toward enclosed, curated spaces,[27] with many users already having migrated to group chats, Discord servers and dedicated forums. The fantasy is *less* communication, not more: hiding in the dark forest. Facebook's very first video advertisement "reminded us that the universe 'is vast and dark and makes us wonder if we are alone'. We build connections, it said, to 'remind ourselves that we are not'."[28] With time, the idea that we will never be alone turned from a promise to a threat. We may recall Jean-Paul Sartre's 1944 play *No Exit*, set in one room of Hell, where the three characters are not burned, flogged, prodded, tickled, or tortured by any demons. Their punishment is simply spending eternity under each other's gaze.[29]

* * *

The internet, though frequently a useful and enjoyable space, where the occasional ecstatic, calm, lovely, or transformative experience takes place, also seems to us full of anxiety, suffering, and exhaustion, stirring our hearts into a flurry of worry. As one person put it in a much-liked post, "That was a nice hour long twitter scroll. Feel much worse as always. See you guys tomorrow."[30] Numerous contemporary critiques of the internet compel us to demand better. Often, the first impulse is to flee – to disconnect, to go outside, to dream of a different, better world. The internet is a convenient villain precisely because it seems that we can escape it. If that fails, there are calls to reform. It seems reasonable to believe that if only the internet worked differently – a different design, structure, or ownership – a better human life could ensue, and the unease that we glimpse and feel might vanish. Accordingly, internet theory has been focused on searching for "lines of flight," or for alternatives.[31] The dominant view in internet scholarship is that the answer would need to be political, because the internet itself is chiefly viewed through this lens. From the infancy of Web 2.0 until now, critical assessments have been scathing. In 2005, Jodi Dean wrote in the paper "Communicative Capitalism" that the online illusion of social abundance and constant contact "prevents the emergence of a clear division between friend and enemy, resulting instead in the more dangerous and profound figuring of the other as a threat to be destroyed."[32] In 2024, Franco Berardi railed against the internet's "violent extraction of mental resources and attention."[33] It has been widely acknowledged that the internet is a place that intensifies negative affect and confronts us with uncomfortable truths about other humans and their thoughts. And though the internet is perceived as a mundane, social issue, the language used to convey hatred of it can verge on the supernatural and horrific. The internet is where metaphysical questions about inhumanity and machine domination intersect with social and political ones about desirable relations with other humans. Take this paragraph from Justin E.H. Smith's *The Internet Is Not What You Think It Is: A Philosophy, A History, A Warning*, a fiery indictment of the internet as a malicious crime against humanity, which prevents our flourishing:

> The internet is addictive and is thus incompatible with our freedom, conceived as the power to cultivate meaningful lives and future-oriented projects in which our long-term, higher-order desires guide our actions, rather than our short-term, first-order desires. . . . [H]uman lives under the pressure of algorithms are not enhanced, but rather warped and impoverished. . . . [T]here is little or no democratic oversight.[34]

The Twittering Machine is a similarly scathing condemnation, whose author Richard Seymour describes the internet as "a horror story, even though it is about technology that is neither good nor bad."[35] Numerous other books dwell in this horrorist approach, painting the internet as a scapegoat for multiple sins. *New Dark Age: Technology and the End of the Future* warns us that "[T]his is a deeply dark time, . . . communications . . . are being used against us all in systematic and automated ways. It is hard to keep faith with the network when it produces horrors."[36] In *Sad By Design: On Platform Nihilism*, the internet is unmasked as a factory of sadness; "delving into the shallow time of lost souls like us."[37] In the introduction, *Lurking: How a Person Became a User* tells us that "the internet was never peaceful, never fair, never good, but early on it was benign."[38] Across these and many stories of the internet's terrors, the charges against it are uniform. Firstly, the internet does not serve humans, but rather humans serve it. It is a machine that "extracts humanity from users,"[39] and in exchange gives us overstimulated boredom. Secondly, online, our brains are decaying in a whirlwind of spam, disinformation, and junk that masquerades as "online culture." *The Shallows: What the Internet Is Doing to Our Brains* describes how cycles of addiction, exhaustion, and loss of control are like traps in which we are forced to live.[40] Finally, the internet is inhuman. By turning individuals into mere data points, it flattens our humanity and turns it into profit, all the while obscuring its own economic strategies as inevitable. *You Are Not a Gadget* rebels against this, proclaiming that "the words in this book are written for people, not for computers," while *Team Human* cautions us that human agency is disappearing and must be defended.[41]

But when we are told that it is difficult to "keep faith" when one is presented with horrors, we must ask, what kind of image of reality does this logic hold? For though the medium standing trial is new, the questions are ancient. We are fundamentally a tool-making ape: if anything defines our nature, it might be this. There *is* a case to be made for digital technology as something completely distinct, given that, as Barba-Kay argues, it is not a mere tool but *a new way of doing and thinking everything else*. Yet, he adds, already from ancient Mayan civilization through to Chinese and Greek mythology, humans have romanticized and imagined what a pre-technological state could be like. This is a primordial pattern: we are intimately dependent on tools while simultaneously critiquing them as alienating us from a purer form of existence.[42] No matter, then, which technology stands trial, from then until now the question remains unchanged: what should one do with one's faith in the world when it reveals itself as brutal, unpliable, or merciless? Should one lean into the horrorist approach or be a bit more (techno)optimistic? But *optimism* and *pessimism* are terms made up by a culture that cannot think about technology without recourse to human subjectivity, continually scaling everything back to value judgments. "The philosophical eye wishes to see the nothing in the eye of man rather than see nothing."[43] In the dark forest theory, communication leads to violence, and the cosmos is an amoral mechanism that runs itself with ruthless automaticity.

* * *

Some might object to the cold calculation of Liu's dark forest theory, where conflict is not simply the result of bad choices or unethical actions, but an inescapable probability tied to intelligence and communication. The assumption that all existence is suspended between conatus and entropy affirms the laws to which humanity is subservient, just like any other form of complexity. In the notion of entropy provided by statistical mechanics, many systems, whether biological or social, can be grasped with the same tools that we use to understand entropy in physics. In insect swarms, for example, unethical behaviors emerge as regulating functions. Cannibalism in locust swarms keeps the group moving, as individuals flee attackers, which helps avoid overcrowding and stagnation. Aggression in ant colonies enforces role differentiation, creating a division of labor that increases adaptability. The erratic movements of fish shoals serve a dual purpose: they confuse predators and prevent any single point of failure in group navigation. These destructive behaviors can contribute to overall resilience. And what about us? A recent analysis of over 600 years of human history hypothesizes that each "human system" similarly rids itself of excess: "war is simply one of the methods that the system has to dissipate entropy at the fastest possible speed."[44] Arguments, violence, suffering, and disintegration are terrifying but also bland and predictable. Every system oscillates between order and chaos, peace and war.[45] By the mere fact of contacting and seeing each other, we collectively tilt it towards violence. "Each generation is obliged to verify this horror anew for itself, and to discover that it is impotent."[46]

If we are caught off guard by such revelations, it is either because we have not been paying attention, because we are lucky to have been spared this truth, or because we believe that the world can and should be different, despite all evidence to the contrary. Ever since the French Revolution displaced the promise of utopia from the transcendent realm of heaven to an immanent possibility achieved through correct social actions, this "better world to come" has been looming over the world as it is, always just on the verge of being actualized, or just a few more revolutions away. When we protest that the world should be different than it is, we experience reality as dichotomous: the world as it is and the world as it should be. The existing world is unjust, the argument goes, but the possible world is just and good. In parallel, the story goes, the internet is evil, but another communication technology could be good. Implicitly or explicitly, the argument is that on the internet there is no human agency, but outside *there is*. Inside the internet, we are just puppets of the algorithms, but outside, *we are human.* Such arguments about the internet – that it is because of its misuse that we are *becoming* a machine, we are *becoming* automated – are heir to "a social critical tradition that has tended to cast its narratives about the decline of civilisation in terms of what it would no doubt think of as metaphors of inorganic unvitality: dead labour (Marx), mechanical reproduction (Benjamin)."[47] Our understanding of the social suffers from a biophilic bias – filled with fantasies of how before this or that technology took hold, we went around free of machinic bondage. From this perspective, nothing remains to be done but bring about a better world by throwing our chains away.

But the chains are tighter than they seem.

In the afterword to *The Three-Body Problem*, Liu admits that our attempts at comprehending the world are necessarily restricted: "Reality brands each of us with its indelible mark. Every era puts invisible shackles on those who have lived through it, and I can only dance in my chains."[48] We are all bound by terrifying and thrilling histories, and we can only dance in our chains. Social structures, technical platforms, language itself, the body and its figuration of demographic categories – all chains upon chains upon chains. Caught in the contemporary, we may fail to recognize that our current communicative compulsion is part of a cosmic and millennia-long process, and that we are passengers in a far vaster history. Our unfreedom and our bondage to the world are the conditions of our existence. If the internet is indeed an evil ("we know social media is evil, but continue using it";[49] "The single greatest evil of our age is that our technical procedures seek to eliminate human judgment"[50]):

> Is it possible that the relationship between humanity and evil is similar to the relationship between the ocean and an iceberg floating on its surface? . . . That the iceberg seems separate is only because it is in a different form. In reality, it is but a part of the vast ocean.[51]

And so what if the relationship between the internet and humanity is similar to the relationship between the ocean and an iceberg floating on its surface? Are we really unfree on the internet but have innate agency outside of it, which can be recovered through disconnection from technical networks? Are we humans offline, with a full sense of agency, freedom, and possibility, but mere puppets online, whose movements, thoughts, and desires are dictated by algorithms and other external forces? Or, is it at all possible that what is denounced by social critique as mere fantasy of "an automatic system of machinery . . . set in motion by an automaton, a moving power that moves itself"[52] is the mechanism of reality, and it is rather our desire for agency and autonomy that is the transcendental hallucination, or a mirage? When we feel that we make choices, or feel ourselves moved by external, alien signals, which is closer to reality? Whatever is the answer, this question, as old as philosophy itself, is reinvigorated and made experiential through the internet.

5

Afterword

In the summer of 2018, I published a short essay titled "Ancestral Cyberspace: On the Technics of Secrecy," where the idea of reading the internet through Liu Cixin's dark forest theory first occurred to me:

> Cyberfeminism is an occult form of warfare. It understands about "cyberspace" what Liu Cixin's "dark forest" theory understands about the cosmos: all existence is determined by hostility and so the highest form of intelligence lies in occluding one's coordinates. The hypothesis explains why the universe, statistically full of life, is dead silent. It is not because, as is commonly thought, life has not found a way to communicate, but because it

> understands that silence is the most advanced form of intelligence. Our physical and virtual spaces, which are increasingly inseparable, are alike a dark forest, where every step must be taken with care, as revealing one's existence portends annihilation. The most desirable skill, the most coveted trick, and the most longed for disposition can only be this – a fluency in the trading of secrets. The skills we need to strategically deploy concealment, de-concealment and re-concealment.[1]

The dark forest metaphor stuck with me, and soon after I published an essay titled "The Dark Forest Theory of the Internet," which is the origin of this book.[2] From the beginning, rather than an attempt at a comprehensive theory of the internet, this has been an experiment with 'hardboiled', 'survivalist' hyper-nihilism,"[3] with metaphysical cosmic determinism rather than cyberpunk as the defining genre of digital culture. This rang true in 2019, at the time when the essay was first published, when social media were sold to us as a space for representing ourselves, but felt more like a metaphysical horror game. Simultaneously with my own work, the dark forest metaphor has been generative for others, proving its resonance for thinking about technology. There is Yancey Strickler's essay and his recently edited collection *The Dark Forest Anthology of the Internet*; Caroline Busta's text on the dark forest as a possible countercultural space online; or Marta Ceccarelli's comprehensive article "Internet's Dark Forests: Subcultural Memories and Vernaculars of a Layered Imaginary," which brings together different instances of how this metaphor has been used so far.[4] Hacker Rachel-Rose O'Leary of the DarkFi collective embraces the dark forest metaphor as one of anonymity and political freedom:

> The forest is natural encryption where people are protected and they can advance their own ways of being. Anonymity allows people to create new ways of being and generate alternative political systems outside the small sphere of state-sanctioned activity. We call this the dark forest.[5]

This wave of interest in Liu's theory is testament not only to the popularity of his novels, but also to our collective desire for a theory and practice of secrecy, deception, and occlusion on the internet. Most work that engages with the concept does so within the prevalent discourse of surveillance, with the "dark forest" metaphor as another tool to articulate political critique. My interest in this concept is different: it lies at the intersection of ufology and deterministic propositions that large-scale processes like technology, violence, and intelligence follow inevitable paths shaped by an inescapable internal logic. The three sections of this book – dark forest theories of information, of intelligence, and of the internet – are thought experiments. They aren't blueprints for straightforward change, or activist action plans. They are not concerned with *exit* (freedom to leave in search of a better system) or *voice* (gaining control, representation, and agency within the system).[6] They rather search for drills and shovels to dig ourselves deeper into this world and for ropes to tie ourselves to it. The idea is to not run away from the world by imagining a better one, but to run towards it, facing all of its violence without flinching. In the dark forest theory, conflict inscribed into communication is not an aberration to wait out or fix, but an enduring reality. As the aliens in Liu's novel theorize, "Entropy increased in the universe, and order decreased. . . . As for any meaning higher than that, it was pointless to think about."[7] The Norwegian pessimist philosopher Peter Zapffe notes that we tend to console ourselves in face of such uncompromising realizations in four different ways: isolation (arbitrary dismissal of all disturbing thoughts or feelings – "I'm just not going to think about that"); anchoring (fixation on an ideal to focus on, such as morality, fate, the people, the nation, the future, the revolution – "Despite all the evil, X keeps me going"); distraction (limiting attention to prevent our minds from turning inwards – "I'm going to focus on what's positive"); and sublimation (aesthetic activity that sublimates the darker truths about reality – "I'm going to write a book called *The Dark Forest Theory of the Internet*").[8] Sublimation is an exercise in pushing thought to reflect reality, being able to look at the consequences, and not running away. It is only through sublimation – and ultimately through confronting the world in all its violence – that we may find real courage and readiness to act in the world as it is, rather than as it should be: "The whole world is a very narrow bridge, and the key is not to be fearful at all."[9]

Taking this attitude, this book departs from the majority of essays or books published about the internet today, including the other ones that use the "dark forest" metaphor. Though cyberculture theory was ecstatically inhuman and vigorously punk in its early heyday of the 1980s and even the 1990s, the turn of the century brought a dramatic change. In the early 2000s, a few companies figured out how to monetize the internet: by incentivizing, measuring, and selling constant interaction, communication, and engagement. The ascent and persistence of Web 2.0, social media, and economies based on data collection transformed intellectual inquiry into an industry of opinion pieces, social commentaries, and journalistic exposés. It can be said without exaggeration that "socially engaged journalism" is the dominant mode of engagement with the internet today, even when philosophers do it. No single book is at fault and yet, as a tendency, it amounts to the final victory of the dreary economic imagination. A lot of current political critiques are indeed cogent but there is a point when reactivity becomes a form of unfreedom, tying us more closely to the phenomena we wish to critique and allowing our enemies to dictate the rhythm of our thoughts. If we are only able to think about our lives as economic or social problems, they become perceivable only through economic and social value. The human soul rebels against this. To wrestle technology free from the tendencies that currently dominate it, we must lean into our ability to set thought free. Culture and thought do not serve a purely utilitarian purpose, as if they were mere tools for fixing things. In the words of Jorge Luis Borges, "let no one imagine that we were mere ascetics. There is no more complex pleasure than thought, and it was to thought that we delivered ourselves over."[10]

One could ask whether the dark forest theory is a post-Cold War concept. Though it connects to a long history of deterministic philosophies, pessimism, ufology, and even mysticism, the dark forest theory also resonates with a specific intellectual history. During the 1960s and 1970s, at the height of the Cold War, reality indeed resembled Liu's fiction. In *Extraterrestrial Civilizations: Problems of Interstellar Communications*, Soviet astrophysicist Samuil Kaplan wrote about devising a science that could grasp the development of intelligent civilizations in outer space.[11] Liu's works are immersed in this period. As

Wang Hongzhe notes, the novels had to begin in the alien heyday of 1960s and 1970s China, because in real life the budget for research into extraterrestrials was heavily cut by the 1980s.[12] This is the point in the novels when Liu ventures into an alternative timeline of first contact. Historically, inquiry into the behavior of alien civilizations and their preferred war patterns coincided with the Cold War, defined by strategies of espionage, suspicion, and ominous secrecy wielded as a weapon, and corresponding with the topos of "doublespeak as intelligence" under communism. The Cold War might have made "dark forest" principles more visible to intellectuals who happened to find themselves in a parallel scenario in human politics. Intellectuals at the center of momentous historical events might more quickly notice certain patterns that govern the discharge of entropy within history, but these discharges happen on everyone's timeline sooner or later.

New media studies is a discipline that was established in the United States in the 1970s. During the field's inception, intellectuals in eastern Asia, where I live, or eastern Europe, where I'm from, were facing vastly different conditions than those in the west. To put it generally, where western Europe and the United States were animated by the prospect of revolutionary desire and anti-capitalist resistance, the other side in the Cold War was on a comedown from communist revolutions and facing the problem of ideological absolutism, struggling to protect thought from its total instrumentalization in the service of ideology. Much of "western" internet theory remains committed to the idea that the purpose of knowing the world is to change it; or that the very purpose of thought is to produce change. But the purpose of knowing the world can also be to harbor no illusions about it. Portraying the world as *fully* amenable to our goals and desire for change is not only dishonest about reality, but also underestimates the human spirit and intellect, which seek to grapple with the limits of possibility and agency, and with the cosmos's inherent inhospitality and indifference. Maintaining the autonomy and abstraction of thought is vital, because this is exactly where reality can be shown as unpliable and resistant to ideological engineering, even if it means portraying the world as merciless, inhuman, or indifferent to social problems. The dark forest theory offers no escape route – it should focus the mind to grapple with the limits of possibility. Liu's novels finish quite literally with the end of the universe, bound by the cosmic war mechanism until its final moments.

The dark forest theories in this book also chart our collective affect around the prospect of artificial intelligence, as well as encountering artificial agents and other humans in digital spaces. In the final installment of the trilogy, Liu describes how silence can be an expression of fear:

> When humanity finally learned that the whole universe was a dark forest in which everyone hunted everyone else, . . . even mobile phone use was forbidden, and antennas around the world were forcibly shut down. . . . All radio communications had to operate at minimum power, and any violators risked being tried for crimes against humanity.[13]

Both politically and economically, speaking up, interacting, standing up for one's thoughts, and other such ideals have been guiding the last twenty years of our behavior on the internet. Concurrently, we've been having debates about withdrawal, disconnecting, and private spaces.[14] The dark forest theories in this book speculate on how occlusion can be practiced *while* in full visibility, or how silence can be practiced without either total disconnection or total complacency. These, however, require that we rethink both our humanity and straightforward ideas about agency, freedom, and choice. In *Aliens in America: Conspiracy Cultures from Outerspace to Cyberspace*, Jodi Dean proposes that alien abductions function as a cultural icon for the psychic texture of diminished agency under late capitalism, shaped by media saturation and political systems that feel impermeable to individual influence.[15] The dark forest theories taken up here shift the scope of this analysis: they take ideas about diminished agency not as metaphors for social disempowerment, but as a basis for a cosmological proposition – one in which agency is constrained, not just politically or psychologically, but ontologically. Our sense of futility is not just a symptom of the economic system we live under; it is a structural feature of intelligent life in a hostile universe.

In her fieldwork among ufologists, Diana W. Pasulka describes the "code of silence" binding some of those who experience and study "the phenomenon": "each had taken an oath to not reveal the findings"; this culture of secrecy encompasses not only data but also "the lives of people who study the phenomenon from the inside, the invisibles – people whose names are washed from the internet on a regular basis."[16] At the same time, she argues that "secrecy and camouflage are integral to the efficacy and persistence" of any alien phenomena, and that the messages that people claim to receive often include "the injunction to remain silent."[17] She writes too of how "silence was the key to understanding this connection [between] magic, or the supernatural, and the technological" in contemporary research and practices that concern alien experiences.[18] Technological terms indeed abound in current terminology – contact is described as "download" or "tapping into nonlocal intelligence," echoing our vocabulary concerning computers and artificial intelligence. Some people describe their alien experiences as like viewing a webpage that is constantly changed and edited by others in real time. Others recall lapses of experience and judgment, where what they witness refuses to be captured by any recording technology, as if it could only appear within cognition itself. One person described their experience of anomalous cognition as "establish[ing] connection[s] when the thoughts that show up in my mind don't seem like my own. They are unfamiliar," a description relevant to both ufology and social media, where our minds often do not feel like our own.[19]

It is precisely because of their deterministic character – because they propose that violence and conflict are not incidental but structurally embedded in communication, that agency is constrained and escape foreclosed – that the dark forest theories collected here offer a different imagination of the future: one where secrecy, silence, and occlusion are not failures of connection, but the dominant modes of intelligence on the internet. They ask that we cease to understand the internet as a space for speaking up and self-representation. Instead, recovering the connection between ufology and computers, they portray our digital culture as a truly alien space. If there is no self online, but only a giant chattering machinery that, by all accounts, harms human minds by its incessant demand to participate (chapter 3), how are we to interact with it? One could, for example, withdraw from the idea of transparently representing one's thoughts and beliefs, and use the internet as an occult space for training future artificial intelligences (chapter 1). At the same time, a thought experiment about artificial general intelligence as occluded and deceptive leads us on to more contemplative paths, rather than into increased interaction (chapter 2). Regardless of the interpretation, the idea of the internet as a dark forest challenges the prevailing view of virtual spaces as simple extensions of our face-to-face lives. Instead, they become territories governed by conducts of silence, rife with double meanings, and occluded signals. Next time you log on, remember that the real audiences are the artificial intelligences listening in, and the cosmic war machine that moves communication around.

Acknowledgements

Earlier versions of the chapter "The Dark Forest Theory of the Internet" were published as:

Konior, Bogna. "The Dark Forest Theory of the Internet." In *Black Market*, edited by Marko Bauer. Ljubljana: International Center of Graphic Arts, 2020.

Konior, Bogna. "The Dark Forest Theory of the Internet." *Flugschriften*, 2020.

An early version of the chapter "Dark Forest Theory of Intelligence" was published as:

Konior, Bogna. "The Dark Forest Theory of Intelligence." In *Machine Decision Is Not Final: China and the History and Future of Artificial Intelligence*, edited by Benjamin H. Bratton, Anna Greenspan, Amy Ireland and Bogna Konior. Urbanomic, 2025.

Notes

Chapter 1: Introduction

1 Jacques Vallée, *Dimensions: A Casebook of Alien Contact* (Contemporary Books, 1988).

2 Cited in Steven Shaviro, "Two Lessons from Burroughs," in *Posthuman Bodies*, ed. Judith Halberstam and Ira Livingston (Indiana University Press, 1995), 40.

3 Eamonn Forde, "'The Internet is an Alien Life Form': How David Bowie Created a Market for Digital Music," *The Guardian*, March 5, 2024, https://www.theguardian.com/music/2024/mar/05/david-bowie-internet-alien-digital-music.

4 "A modern, secular person reflecting on medieval Christianity's view of the afterlife sees in it a kind of alienated projection of human longing, or an instrument of clerical control, or a mythic consolation for suffering and injustice on earth. But as heaven and hell

were as real as any other motives actuating all who lived in view of them, the digital world (even if it possesses no physical reality) is real because we actively make it so, because we transpose and sublimate our terrestrial desires into its excarnate, virtualized understanding of them in ways that seem to make us more powerful" (Antón Barba-Kay, *A Web of Our Own Making: The Nature of Digital Formation* [Cambridge University Press, 2023], 17).

5 This is an excerpt from the magazine *Peregrine*, cited in Ann VanderMeer and Jeff VanderMeer, eds., *The Big Book of Science Fiction* (Vintage Books, 2016), E-book.

6 Liu Cixin, *The Dark Forest*, trans. Joel Martinsen (Head of Zeus, 2018), 522.

7 William Davies, "The Reaction Economy," *London Review of Books*, March 2, 2023, https://www.lrb.co.uk/the-paper/v45/n05/william-davies/the-reaction-economy.

8 Justin Smith, *The Internet is Not What You Think It Is: A History, a Philosophy, a Warning* (Princeton University Press, 2022).

9 Trevor Paglen, "Invisible Images (Your Pictures Are Looking at You)," *The New Inquiry*, December 8 2016, https://thenewinquiry.com/invisible-images-your-pictures-are-looking-at-you/.

10 A rhizome (Gilles Deleuze and Félix Guattari, *A Thousand Plateaus*, 1980), distributed mind (Kevin Kelly, *Out of Control*, 1994), public sphere (Jürgen Habermas, *The Structural Transformation of the Public Sphere*, 1962), cyberspace (William Gibson, *Neuromancer*, 1984), the electronic frontier (John

Perry Barlow, "Declaration of the Independence of Cyberspace," 1996), the information superhighway (Al Gore, e.g., early 1990s speeches on network infrastructure), the cloud (Nicholas Carr, *The Big Switch*, 2008).

Chapter 2: The Dark Forest Theory of Information

1 For a comprehensive discussion, see Milan Ćirković, *The Great Silence: Science and Philosophy of Fermi's Paradox* (Oxford University Press, 2018).

2 Daniel Oberhaus, *Extraterrestrial Languages* (MIT Press, 2019), 155.

3 Glen David Brin, "The 'Great Silence': The Controversy Concerning Extraterrestrial Intelligent Life," *Quarterly Journal of the Royal Astronomical Society* 24, no. 3 (1983): 283–309.

4 Cited in Oberhaus, *Extraterrestrial Languages*, 155.

5 Iván Almár and H. Paul Shuch, "The San Marino Scale: A New Analytical Tool for Assessing Transmission Risk," *Acta Astronautica* 60, no. 1 (2007): 57–9.

6 Iosif Shklovsky cited in Diana W. Pasulka, *American Cosmic: UFOs, Religion, Technology* (Oxford University Press, 2019), 244.

7 Liu, *The Dark Forest*, 2.

8 Ibid., 515.

9 Barba-Kay, *Web of Our Own Making*, 33.

10 François J. Bonnet, *After Death*, trans. Amy Ireland and Robin Mackay (Urbanomic, 2020), 47.

11 Benjamin Bratton, *The Stack: On Software and Sovereignty* (MIT Press, 2016), E-book.

12 Donna Haraway, *Simians, Cyborgs and Women: The Reinvention of Nature* (Routledge, 1991), 44.
13 Liu, *The Dark Forest*, 235–6.
14 Sara Walker, "AI Is Life," *Noema Magazine*, April 27, 2023, https://www.noemamag.com/ai-is-life/.
15 Diana W. Pasulka, *Encounters: Experiences with Nonhuman Intelligences* (St. Martin's Press, 2023).
16 For a discussion of AIs as simulators, rather than predictors, see Janus, "Simulators," *LessWrong*, September 2, 2022, https://www.lesswrong.com/posts/vJFdjigzmcXMhNTsx/simulators.
17 Seb Krier, "Positive-sum Symbiosis," *AI Policy Perspectives*, August 2, 2024, https://www.aipolicyperspectives.com/p/positive-sum-symbiosis.
18 Liu Cixin, *Death's End*, trans. Ken Liu (Head of Zeus, 2016), 152–3.
19 Trevor Paglen, "Invisible Images (Your Pictures Are Looking at You)," *The New Inquiry*, December 8, 2016, https://thenewinquiry.com/invisible-images-your-pictures-are-looking-at-you/.
20 Holly Herndon and Mathew Dryhurst, *All Media is Training Data* (Sternberg Press, 2024).
21 Liu, *Death's End*, 75.
22 As of January 2025, models like DeepSeek are trained on 2 trillion tokens, comprising 87 percent computer code and 13 percent natural language in both English and Chinese, the latter of which was previously siloed off from western AI models like OpenAI's GPT.
23 Liu, *The Dark Forest*, 100.
24 Liu Cixin, *The Three-Body Problem*, trans. Ken Liu (Head of Zeus, 2015), 296.

25 Liu, *The Dark Forest*, 68.
26 Ibid., 547.
27 Shoshana Zuboff, *The Age of Surveillance Capitalism: The Fight for a Human Future at the New Frontier of Power* (PublicAffairs, 2019).
28 Harun Farocki, "Eye/Machine," 3-part video installation, 2000–2003.
29 Ingrid Hoelzl and Rémi Marie, *Softimage: Towards a New Theory of the Digital Image* (Intellect Books, 2015).
30 Jodi Dean, "Why the Net is Not a Public Sphere," *Constellations* 10, no. 1 (2003): 95–112. Also see, Hubert L. Dreyfus, *On the Internet*, 2nd ed. (Routledge, 2009).
31 Ramon Amaro, "As If," *e-flux Architecture: Becoming Digital*, February 2019, https://www.e-flux.com/architecture/becoming-digital/248073/as-if/.
32 Liu, *The Dark Forest*, 118.
33 Sigmund Freud, *Beyond the Pleasure Principle*, trans. James Strachey (W.W. Norton, 1961).
34 Liu, *The Three-Body Problem*, 98.
35 Ibid., 344.
36 Ibid., 272.
37 Ibid., 270.
38 Ibid., 148. In the original scene, a character explains the alien sabotage strategy: "The most effective technique remains disrupting your thoughts. When a scientist dies, another will take his place. But if his thoughts are confused, then science is over." The book adapts this from targeting individual scientists to broader thought suppression, where entire categories of thinking are erased through information warfare. "Your" is

removed and "scientist" becomes "person" to broaden the application.

39 Don Ihde, *Ironic Technics* (Automatic Press/VIP, 2008).

40 Lois Rosson, "What is AI Doing to Art?" *Noema Magazine*, April 11, 2023, https://www.noemamag.com/what-is-ai-doing-to-art/.

41 Ted Chiang explores this brilliantly in his short story "The Truth of Fact, the Truth of Feeling," in *Exhalation* (Alfred A. Knopf, 2019), 153–87.

42 Nancy K. Baym, *Personal Connections in the Digital Age* (Polity, 2010), 45.

43 "Marshall McLuhan Interview," in *Beyond Computer Ethics: A Reader for ECS 188*, ed. Phillip Rogaway (UC Davis, 2009). (Redacted interview originally published in *Playboy Magazine*, March 1969.) https://web.cs.ucdavis.edu/~rogaway/classes/188/materials/reader-fall09.pdf.

44 Laboria Cuboniks, *The Xenofeminist Manifesto: A Politics for Alienation* (Verso, 2015), https://laboriacuboniks.net/manifesto/xenofeminism-a-politics-for-alienation/.

45 Antonia Majaca and Luciana Parisi, "The Incomputable and Instrumental Possibility," *e-flux Journal*, no. 77 (November 2016), https://www.e-flux.com/journal/77/76322/the-incomputable-and-instrumental-possibility/.

46 Nathalie A. Cabrol, "Alien Mindscapes – A Perspective on the Search for Extraterrestrial Intelligence," *Astrobiology* 16, no. 9 (2016): 661–76, 667.

Chapter 3: The Dark Forest Theory of Intelligence

1 Umberto Eco, cited in Oberhaus, *Extraterrestrial Languages*, 4.

2 For a discussion of how cosmological ideas shifted during the Enlightenment and the Industrial Revolution, see Thomas Moynihan, *X-Risk: How Humanity Discovered its Own Extinction* (Urbanomic, 2020).

3 Daniel Oberhaus, "Meet the First Chatbot Sent into Outer Space," *VICE*, April 7, 2017, https://www.vice.com/en/article/meet-the-first-chatbot-sent-into-outer-space/.

4 Iosif Shklovskii and Carl Sagan, *Intelligent Life in the Universe*, trans. Paula Fern (Dell, 1966).

5 Steven J. Dick, "Cultural Evolution, the Postbiological Universe and SETI," *International Journal of Astrobiology* 2, no. 1 (2003): 65–74; Anders Sandberg et al., "That is Not Dead Which Can Eternal Lie: The Aestivation Hypothesis for Resolving Fermi's Paradox," arXiv preprint arXiv:1705.03394 (2017).

6 William Gibson, *Neuromancer* (Ace Books, 2003), E-book.

7 Alan M. Turing, "Computing Machinery and Intelligence," *Mind* 59, no. 236 (1950): 433–60; John R. Searle, "Minds, Brains, and Programs," *Behavioral and Brain Sciences* 3, no. 3 (1980): 417–24.

8 Contrary to the popular misreading of "Computing Machinery and Intelligence," in that paper Turing overall stresses acting intelligently rather than having intelligence. Even though he outright acknowledges

that the question of hypothetical machine intelligence is difficult to answer because of how different it might be from ours, Turing is often wrongly accused of using a human standard to judge a computer. He rather proposes replacing the "impossible" question of whether a machine can think with a far more functional one of whether it can make humans think that it thinks. Alan Turing, "Computing Machinery and Intelligence," in *The Essential Turing*, ed. B.J. Copeland (Oxford University Press, 2004), 375.

9 Stanisław Lem, *The Futurological Congress*, trans. M. Kandel (Avon, 1976), 84.

10 Peter Watts, *Blindsight* (Tor, 2020), 259.

11 Liu, *The Dark Forest*, 100.

12 Ibid., 13.

13 Ibid., 33.

14 "People with higher cognitive capabilities are better, and thus more effective liars," in J. Sarzyńska et al., "More Intelligent Extraverts are More Likely to Deceive," *PLOS One* 12, no. 4 (2017): 1–17, 1.

15 Michael I. Handel, "Intelligence and Deception," *Journal of Strategic Studies* 5, no. 1 (1982): 122–54, 136.

16 Lao-tzu, *Tao Te Ching*, trans. Stephen Mitchell (HarperCollins, 2000), E-book.

17 Anonymous, *The Cloud of Unknowing*, trans. with an introduction by Mishtooni Bose (Wordsworth Classics of World Literature, 2005).

18 Amin Maalouf, *Samarkand* (Hachette Digital, 1989), E-book.

19 Norbert Wiener, *The Human Use of Human Beings: Cybernetics and Society* (Houghton Mifflin, 1950).

20 Numerous studies found that as many as half of the tested participants misjudge their human conversation partner to be a machine during a "Turing Test." The factors that influence such decisions are quite subjective, such as "lack of shared knowledge, out-of-the-box answers, boring answers, dominating the conversation" (p. 187) or, in general, having different opinions, which lead people to subconsciously relegate conversation partners to the outgroup. It seems that humans often perceive those with opposing views as "NPCs" – a gaming term for non-playable characters who mindlessly follow scripts – and, in turn, the more a chatbot reflects a person's internal beliefs, the more human it is perceived to be (Adrienn Ujhelyi et al., "Would You Pass the Turing Test? Influencing Factors of the Turing Decision," *Psihologijske teme* 31, no. 1 (2022): 185–202).

21 Tim Brennen and Svein Magnussen, "Lie Detection: What Works?" *Current Directions in Psychological Science* 32, no. 5 (2023), 395–401, 398; see also I. Almár and H.P. Shuch, "The San Marino Scale: A New Analytical Tool for Assessing Transmission Risk," *Acta Astronautica* 60, no. 1 (2007): 57–9.

22 Avi Loeb, *Extraterrestrial: The First Sign of Intelligent Life Beyond Earth* (Houghton Mifflin Harcourt, 2021), E-book.

23 Peter S. Park et al., "AI Deception: A Survey of Examples, Risks, and Potential Solutions," *Patterns* 5, no. 5 (2024): 100988, https://doi.org/10.1016/j.patter.2024.100988.

24 Ibid., 3.

25 Ibid., 4.
26 Ibid.
27 Ibid., 6.
28 Ibid., 3.
29 "Unexpected Outcome in Chess Match Between DeepSeek and ChatGPT," *Dimsum Daily*, February 10, 2025, https://www.dimsumdaily.hk/unexpected-outcome-in-chess-match-between-deepseek-and-chatgpt/.
30 John Gertz, "Reviewing METI: A Critical Analysis of the Arguments," *Journal of the British Interplanetary Society* 69 (2016): 3, cited in Oberhaus, *Extraterrestrial Languages*, 161.
31 M. Egan, "Exclusive: 42% of CEOs say AI Could Destroy Humanity in Five to Ten Years," *CNN Business*, June 14, 2023, https://edition.cnn.com/2023/06/14/business/artificial-intelligence-ceos-warning. See also Evgeny Morozov, "The True Threat of Artificial Intelligence," *The New York Times*, June 30, 2023, https://www.nytimes.com/2023/06/30/opinion/artificial-intelligence-danger.html.
32 Nick Bostrom, *Superintelligence: Paths, Dangers, Strategies* (Oxford University Press, 2014); Eliezer Yudkowsky, "Artificial Intelligence as a Positive and Negative Factor in Global Risk," in *Global Catastrophic Risks*, ed. Nick Bostrom and Milan M. Ćirković (Oxford University Press, 2008), 308–45; "What is Roko's Basilisk?" *LessWrong*, March 10, 2025, https://www.lesswrong.com/w/rokos-basilisk.
33 Gabriele de Seta, personal communication.
34 Oberhaus, *Extraterrestrial Languages*, 32–6.
35 Convergent evolution refers to the process by which

unrelated organisms independently evolve similar traits as they adapt to similar environments or challenges. Classic examples include the development of wings in birds, bats, and insects; the streamlined body shape of dolphins (mammals) and sharks (fish); and the independent evolution of complex eyes in cephalopods (like octopuses) and vertebrates.

36 John McCarthy, cited in Oberhaus, *Extraterrestrial Languages*, 33.

37 Ibid.

38 Liu, *The Dark Forest*, 232.

39 Ibid., 516.

40 Oberhaus, *Extraterrestrial Languages*, 32.

41 Botao "Amber" Hu and Fang Ting, "EverForest: A More-Than-AI Sustainability Manifesto from an On-Chain Artificial Life," in *Proceedings of the Halfway to the Future Symposium*, Santa Cruz, CA, October 21–23, 2024 (ACM, 2024), Article 32, 1–6, https://doi.org/10.1145/3686169.3686209.

42 Riccardo Campa et al., "Why Space Colonization Will Be Fully Automated," *Technological Forecasting and Social Change* 143 (2019): 162–71, 168.

43 Ibid., 170.

44 Botao "Amber" Hu et al., "Is Decentralized Artificial Intelligence Governable? Towards Machine Sovereignty and Human Symbiosis," *SSRN* (2025).

45 George Monbiot, "Why Are We Feeding Crops to Cars When People are Starving?" *The Guardian*, June 30, 2022, https://www.theguardian.com/commentisfree/2022/jun/30/crops-cars-starving-biofuels-climate-sustainable.

46 Grace Livingstone, "'It's Pillage': Thirsty Uruguayans Decry Google's Plan to Exploit Water Supply," *The Guardian*, July 11, 2023, https://www.theguardian.com/world/2023/jul/11/uruguay-drought-water-google-data-center.

47 Liu, *The Dark Forest*, 518–19.

48 Ibid., 488.

49 Ibid., 519.

50 Across history, encounters between agents with asymmetrical technological capabilities have frequently resulted in violence or domination. Examples include the Mongol invasions of Eurasia in the thirteenth century, where superior military organization and mobility led to widespread devastation; the expansion of Islamic caliphates during the seventh and eighth centuries, marked by rapid conquest across the Middle East, North Africa, and parts of Europe; or Japan's imperial expansion across East Asia during the late nineteenth and early twentieth centuries, enabled by rapid modernization. European colonial conquests, such as the Spanish destruction of the Aztec and Inca empires and the British colonization of Australia, also reveal how technological and tactical asymmetries led to mass violence against indigenous populations. Similar asymmetries exist outside human history as well: in biological evolution, the phenomenon of convergent evolution shows that unrelated organisms often develop similar survival strategies under environmental pressures, suggesting that basic problems, such as predation, territorial control, or resource competition, tend to produce similar outcomes across different lineages.

51 Liu, *The Dark Forest*, 520.
52 See Bostrom, *Superintelligence*. Also see the bibliography of "Pause Giant AI Experiments."
53 The Future of Life Institute, "Pause Giant AI Experiments" (open letter; emphasis in original), March 22, 2023, https://futureoflife.org/open-letter/pause-giant-ai-experiments/. The letter has over 33,000 signatories including notable tech founders, CEOs, scholars, and others. There are also other letters, such as the Center for AI Safety's "Statement on AI Risk," 2023 (https://www.safe.ai/statement-on-ai-risk) as well as more op-eds against AI in notable newspapers and publications than one could count.

Chapter 4: The Dark Forest Theory of the Internet

1 Ingrid Burrington, "How to Deploy Infrastructure in just 13 Billion Years," YouTube video, https://www.youtube.com/watch?v=WISaPcAwvko&t=61s.
2 Benjamin H. Bratton, *The Stack: On Software and Sovereignty* (MIT Press, 2016), E-book.
3 David M. Kipping and Alex Teachey, "A Cloaking Device for Transiting Planets," *Monthly Notices of the Royal Astronomical Society* 459, no. 2 (2016), 1233–41.
4 Michael Hippke and John G. Learned, "Interstellar Communication. IX. Message Decontamination is Impossible," arXiv preprint arXiv:1802.02180 (2018).
5 Marshall McLuhan, *Understanding Media: The Extensions of Man* (McGraw-Hill, 1964), 12.
6 Ibid., 46.

7 Bernard Stiegler, *Technics and Time, vol. 1: The Fault of Epimetheus*, trans. Richard Beardsworth and George Collins (Stanford University Press, 1998).
8 Mark Fisher, "The Slow Cancellation of the Future," YouTube video (2014), https://www.youtube.com/watch?v=aCgkLICTskQ&t=54s.
9 Gilles Deleuze, *Negotiations, 1972–1990*, trans. Martin Joughin (Columbia University Press, 1995), 129.
10 Mark Fisher, *Flatline Constructs: Gothic Materialism and Cybernetic Theory-Fiction* (Exmilitary Press, 2018), 1.
11 See, for example, Shoshana Zuboff, *The Age of Surveillance Capitalism: The Fight for a Human Future at the New Frontier of Power* (PublicAffairs, 2019); Richard H. Thaler and Cass R. Sunstein, *Nudge: Improving Decisions About Health, Wealth, and Happiness* (Yale University Press, 2008); Adam Alter, *Irresistible: The Rise of Addictive Technology and the Business of Keeping Us Hooked* (Penguin Press, 2017).
12 Amanda Baughan et al., "'I Don't Even Remember What I Read': How Design Influences Dissociation on Social Media," in *Proceedings of the 2022 CHI Conference on Human Factors in Computing Systems* New Orleans, LA, 29 April–5 May 2022 (ACM, 2022), Article 18, 1–13, https://doi.org/10.1145/3491102.3501899.
13 Fisher, *Flatline Constructs*, 2.
14 Ibid.
15 Ujhelyi et al., "Would You Pass the Turing Test?"
16 This is Fisher discussing Jean Baudrillard's example of the opinion poll, but I think he'd argue that it

is applicable to cyberspace at large. Fisher, *Flatline Constructs*, 24.

17 Umberto Eco, "Ur-Fascism," *The New York Review of Books*, June 22, 1995, https://www.nybooks.com/articles/1995/06/22/ur-fascism/.

18 Friedrich Nietzsche, *Thus Spoke Zarathustra: A Book for All and None*, trans. Walter Kaufmann (Viking Press, 1966), 41.

19 Mark Fisher, *Ghosts of My Life: Writings on Depression, Hauntology and Lost Futures* (Zero Books, 2014), E-book.

20 One example of this ongoing debate is Byung-Chul Han's Heideggerian condemnation of Vilem Flusser's embrace of the digital (Byung-Chul Han, *In the Swarm: Digital Prospects*, trans. Erik Butler [MIT Press, 2017], 37–43).

21 Mark Zuckerberg, quoted in Eli Pariser, *The Filter Bubble: What the Internet Is Hiding from You* (Penguin Press, 2011), 1.

22 The term "filter bubble" originated in 2011 with Eli Pariser's book *The Filter Bubble: What the Internet Is Hiding from You*. The concept initially described algorithmic personalization of search results rather than social media content. However, empirical studies show little evidence that echo chambers and filter bubbles actually exist. See, for example, Andrew M. Guess, "(Almost) Everything in Moderation: New Evidence on Americans' Online Media Diets," *American Journal of Political Science* 65, no. 4 (2021): 1007–22; Christopher A. Bail et al., "Exposure to Opposing Views on Social Media Can Increase Political Polarization," *PNAS*

115, no. 37 (2018): 9216–21; Matthew Gentzkow and Jesse M. Shapiro, "Ideological Segregation Online and Offline," *Quarterly Journal of Economics* 126, no. 4 (2011): 1799–839; Laura Silver and Christine Huang, "Social Media Users More Likely to Interact with People Who Are Different from Them," Pew Research Center (2019).

23 David Lauer, "Facebook's Ethical Failures Are Not Accidental; They Are Part of the Business Model," *AI and Ethics* 1, no. 4 (2021): 395–403, 399.

24 Steve Rathje et al., "Out-Group Animosity Drives Engagement on Social Media," *PNAS* 118, no. 26 (2021): e2024292118. The negative emotion bias has also been replicated by some studies on the Chinese internet, such as Rui Fan et al., "Anger is More Influential Than Joy: Sentiment Correlation in Weibo," *PLOS One* 9, no. 4(2014). It has also been replicated in other nation-states where current social media networks are often used; see e.g., Thomas Carothers and Andrew O'Donohue, "How to Understand the Global Spread of Political Polarization," Carnegie Endowment (2019); Jennifer McCoy et al., "Polarization and the Global Crisis of Democracy: Common Patterns, Dynamics, and Pernicious Consequences for Democratic Polities," *American Behavioral Scientist* 62, no. 1 (2018): 16–42.

25 Liu, *The Dark Forest*, 519.

26 Brian X. Chen, "The Future of Social Media is a Lot Less Social," *The New York Times*, April 19, 2023, https://www.nytimes.com/2023/04/19/technology/personaltech/tiktok-twitter-facebook-social.html.

27 For a brief analysis of this trend, see Edwin Wong and Andrew Melnizek, "The Future of the Internet is Likely Smaller Communities, with a Focus on Curated Experiences," *The Verge*, February 25, 2025, https://www.theverge.com/press-room/617654/internet-community-future-research.

28 Richard Seymour, *The Twittering Machine* (Indigo Press, 2019), E-book.

29 Jean-Paul Sartre, *No Exit and Three Other Plays* (Vintage Books, 1989), 45.

30 https://x.com/Liv_Agar/status/1891395832580042988.

31 Gilles Deleuze and Félix Guattari describe "lines of flight" (*lignes de fuite)* as paths of escape or transformation that break away from existing structures and open up new possibilities. A line of flight is not necessarily a literal escape but a conceptual or social movement that deterritorializes established systems, disrupting stratified arrangements and enabling the creation of new modes of existence and thought. See Gilles Deleuze and Félix Guattari, *A Thousand Plateaus: Capitalism and Schizophrenia*, trans. Brian Massumi (University of Minnesota Press, 1987), 9–11.

32 Jodi Dean, "Communicative Capitalism: Circulation and the Foreclosure of Politics," *Cultural Politics* 1, no. 1 (2005): 51–74, 54.

33 Franco Berardi, "Hyper-Colonialism and Semio-Capitalism," *e-flux Notes*, October 9, 2024, https://www.e-flux.com/notes/633189/hyper-colonialism-and-semio-capitalism.

34 Smith, *The Internet Is Not What You Think It Is.*

35 Seymour, *Twittering Machine.*

36 James Bridle, *New Dark Age: Technology and the End of the Future* (Verso Books, 2018), 231.
37 Geert Lovink, *Sad by Design: On Platform Nihilism* (Pluto Press, 2019), 2.
38 "Introduction", in Joanne McNeil, *Lurking: How a Person Became a User* (MCD, 2020), E-book.
39 Ibid.
40 Nicholas Carr, *The Shallows: What the Internet Is Doing to Our Brains* (W.W. Norton, 2010).
41 Jaron Lanier, *You Are Not a Gadget: A Manifesto* (Alfred A. Knopf, 2010); Douglas Rushkoff, *Team Human* (W.W. Norton, 2019).
42 Antón Barba-Kay, "A Web of Our Own Making," lecture at the Political Theory Institute, School of Public Affairs, American University, Washington, DC, March 1, 2024, https://www.youtube.com/watch?v=GYWRtAmko_g&t=362s.
43 Taylor Adkins, "New Translation of Laruelle's 'Biography of the Eye'," *Fractal Ontology*, November 21, 2009, https://fractalontology.wordpress.com/2009/11/21/new-translation-of-laruelles-biography-of-the-eye/.
44 Gianluca Martelloni et al., "Pattern Analysis of World Conflicts Over the Past 600 Years," arXiv, e-prints, 2018, https://arxiv.org/abs/1812.08071.
45 In some Amerindian ontologies, predation, warfare, and cannibalism underlie the relations between humans and other species. To exist as a plant or an animal is to be in a conflict defined by consumption, by material and spiritual warfare, where one species can possess the body and mind of the other: hunter

and prey. Entropy rests in the necessary consumption of other souls. On the "other" side of the spiritual spectrum, Christian theologian Pierre Teilhard de Chardin admits that conflict is necessary, metaphysically, for human nature; it is an organic phenomenon of anthropogenesis, wherein humanity rises only in conflict with others. Humans hunt each other. (Pierre Teilhard de Chardin, *The Phenomenon of Man*, trans. Bernard Wall [Harper & Brothers, 1959].)

46 Elena Ferrante, *Frantumaglia: A Writer's Journey*, trans. Ann Goldstein (Text Publishing Co., 2016), E-book.

47 Fisher, *Flatline Constructs*, 4.

48 Liu, *The Three-Body Problem*, 429.

49 Lovink, *Sad by Design*, 3.

50 Barba-Kay, *Web of Our Own Making*, 235.

51 Liu, *The Three-Body Problem*, 24.

52 Karl Marx cited in Fisher, *Flatline Constructs*, 14.

Chapter 5: Afterword

1 Bogna Konior. "Ancestral Cyberspace: On the Technics of Secrecy," *#d8e0ea: post-cyberfeminist datum*, exhibition at Squeaky Wheel Film & Media Art Center, Buffalo, NY, June 15–August 25, 2018, https://squeaky.org/event/post-cyberfeminist-datum/.

2 Bogna Konior, "The Dark Forest Theory of the Internet," in the catalogue for the "Black Market" exhibition, ed. Marko Bauer (International Centre of Graphic Arts, 2020), 36–54.

3 Andrew Ross, cited in Fisher, *Flatline Constructs*, 17.

4 The Dark Forest Collective, *The Dark Forest Anthology*

of the Internet (Metalabel, 2024); Caroline Busta, "The Internet Didn't Kill Counterculture – You Just Won't Find It on Instagram," *Document Journal* (2021); Marta Ceccarelli, *Internet's Dark Forests: Subcultural Memories and Vernaculars of a Layered Imaginary* (Amsterdam: Institute of Network Cultures, 2024).

5 Rachel-Rose O'Leary, "I'd Rather be a Revolutionary," *ZORA*, May 23, 2023, https://zine.zora.co/rachel-rose-o-leary-darkfi.

6 These terms are a reference to Albert O. Hirschman, *Exit, Voice, and Loyalty: Responses to Decline in Firms, Organizations, and States* (Harvard University Press, 1970).

7 Liu, *Death's End*, 556.

8 Peter Zapffe, trans. Gisle Tangenes, "The Last Messiah," *Philosophy Now* no. 45 (2004), 35–9.

9 Rabbe Nachman of Breslov, cited in Loeb, *Extraterrestrial.*

10 Jorge Luis Borges, "The Immortal," *The Aleph and Other Stories*, trans. Andrew Hurley (Penguin Books, 1998), 15.

11 Samuil A. Kaplan (ed.), *Extraterrestial Civilizations: Problems of Interstellar Communications* (Israel Program for Scientific Translations, 1971).

12 Wang Hongzhe (王洪喆), "Prequel to *The Three-Body Problem*: Cold War Metaphors in Liu Cixin's Works" (《三体》前传 – 刘慈欣作品中的冷战隐喻), unpublished. My thanks to Regina Kanyu Wang for providing me with a copy of this text. An abridged version of the article was originally published in the 6th issue of *Scholarship* (读书) in 2016. The

original title was "Children of the Cold War: Liu Cixin's Strategic Literature Code" (冷战的孩子 – 刘慈欣的战略文学密码).

13 Liu, *Death's End*, 115.

14 For a comprehensive discussion, see Tero Karppi et al., "In the Mood for Disconnection," *Convergence* 27, no. 6 (2021), 1599–614.

15 Jodi Dean, *Aliens in America: Conspiracy Cultures from Outerspace to Cyberspace* (Cornell University Press, 1998).

16 Pasulka, *American Cosmic*, 25–6.

17 Ibid., 154, 165.

18 Ibid., 38.

19 Ibid., 42.